PRAISE FOR *INSPIRATION TO REALIZATION*

"Any woman diving into these stories, taking to heart the insights and applying the wisdom revealed, will know that she can accomplish anything she chooses. She'll also discover that she's part of a very special community of women just like... her. A must read."

— KIM CASTLE, AUTHOR, *WHY BRANDU: BIG BUSINESS SUCCESS NO MATTER YOUR SIZE,* CO-CREATOR OF BRANDU

"*Inspiration to Realization* deeply touches your heart and soul, and through these amazing women's stories, allows you to take pride in your accomplishments. A must-read for any woman who is facing a life challenge."

— DR. CATHERINE CARDINAL, AUTHOR, *A CURE FOR THE COMMON LIFE: THE CARDINAL RULES OF SELF-ESTEEM*

"Self-expression is the most effective strategy for personal and business development on the planet. And this book will teach you how to be fully self-expressed. Inspiring and specific; it is all here. Buy it, read it and use it."

— MICHAEL PORT, BEST-SELLING AUTHOR OF *BOOK YOURSELF SOLID, THE FASTEST, EASIEST, AND MOST RELIABLE SYSTEM FOR GETTING MORE CLIENTS*

"This book will inspire you, make you laugh, and set you on your path to achieving your dreams. A must read for all women."

— STEPHANIE FRANK, AUTHOR, *THE ACCIDENTAL MILLIONAIRE*

"A treasure of good advice, insight and workable solutions from women with fascinating stories who you'll love to meet."

— LINDA SEGER, CONSULTANT, SPEAKER, AUTHOR

"This powerful collection of successful women offers stories that are both inspiring and motivational. Each well crafted chapter will lead you on the path to realizing your own dreams."
— MITCH MEYERSON, AUTHOR, *SIX KEYS TO CREATING THE LIFE YOU DESIRE*

"These women are an inspiration to anyone who wants to find fulfillment using their passion and talents in helping others. This is an awesome resource!"
— BARBARA A.F. GREENE, MASTER CERTIFIED COACH, GREENE AND ASSOCIATES, INC.

"A wonderful collection of wisdom from Wise Women Themselves ... a treasure house of tips on successful and happy living ... a numinous offering of Brilliant Loving Goddess Light and Deep Dark Female Power."
— AVA, DIRECTOR OF THE GODDESS TEMPLE OF ORANGE COUNTY, CALIFORNIA

"*Inspiration to Realization, Volume III* is the volume of transformation. These ladies give us insights into changing our personal, business and financial and spiritual selves. Here they give us the nuts and bolts for a good life, a fulfilled life, an abundant life, your best life now."
— G. MICHAEL SMITH, SPEAKER, TRAINER, CONSULTANT

"What a great feeling it is to know that there are women who have had the same struggles as myself and have come out victors. If they can, then I can; this book has truly inspired me to feel the fear and do it anyway."
— KESHA MCKENZIE, CERTIFIED HOLISTIC HEALTH COUNSELOR, AADP

"Having represented women for over 25 years, this book is an important tool for women of all ages who find themselves for the first time transitioning from married to single life. In order to regain their self-esteem and sense of worthiness, women need to recognize and seize their power through harnessing the important life skills that are contained in this book. I look forward to a world where women understand that they are a significant contributing force in our change and growth as a nation."
— JUDY BOGEN, MATRIMONIAL ATTORNEY, BEVERLY HILLS, CALIFORNIA

"Wow! What an incredible book! I have never seen so many diverse subjects covered with such comprehensive clarity. This book is a must read for anyone looking for a plethora of empowering information for personal and spiritual growth."
— PATRICK HARBULA, AUTHOR, *THE MAGIC OF THE SOUL*

INSPIRATION

— TO —

REALIZATION

VOLUME III

*This book is dedicated
to women who
pursue their dreams.*

INSPIRATION
TO
REALIZATION

VOLUME III

REAL WOMEN
REVEAL PROVEN
STRATEGIES FOR
PERSONAL, BUSINESS,
FINANCIAL AND
SPIRITUAL
FULFILLMENT

COMPILED BY
CHRISTINE KLOSER

Love
Your
Life

Los Angeles, CA

Published by Love Your Life

PO Box 661274, Los Angeles, CA 90066 USA

Published in the US and Canada by Love Your Life

ISBN 10: 0-9664806-5-1
ISBN 13: 978-0-9664806-5-8

Library of Congress Control No: 2004097825

www.LoveYourLife.com
(310) 962-4710

SAN 256-1387

Book Design by Dotti Albertine
Cover Photo by Getty Images

CONTENTS

PART III   SPIRITUAL FULFILLMENT

Introduction

THANK YOU FOR PICKING UP THIS BOOK and reading it! One thing I already know about you is you're a woman with a dream in her heart, and you're willing to do whatever it takes to achieve it!

It has been a great honor to bring together forty-one more voices to share in this third volume of the Inspiration to Realization book series. Voices of women just like you. They reside all across the United States, and most of them have never met each other, yet they share common goals and dreams. They are the same...and they are different. You'll see they have similar insights, stories and strategies to help you live a fulfilling life, but each with a unique twist.

You may notice this book covers a vast range of topics. The reason? I wanted it to reach women from a variety of backgrounds, ages and varied interests. Just like the women in this book who all have their own journey, I know you have your own unique and powerful journey, too. This book is meant to inspire, motivate, educate and encourage you on your path to realizing your dreams.

In today's fast paced world, it has become even more important to nurture every area of your life—personal, business, financial and spiritual. If you focus on business and forget about your personal or family life, then your business success doesn't have much meaning. If you only focus on your spiritual life but don't take responsibility for your financial life, then you'll never experience true freedom. This book is about having it all, and it's written by women who want you to have every dream you desire.

How did these particular women come together on this project? They all "raised their hand" when I put out a request for submissions. They have come together like perfect pieces of a puzzle to help you turn your "inspirations" into "realizations." This book brings together hearts, souls and minds that will touch your heart, resonate in your soul and expand your mind.

As you dive into this book, you may choose to read the chapters in order or simply open to a random page and start anywhere. You may find some chapters do not relate to your current situation, yet when you read it twelve months later, the message may be exactly what you need to hear. Let this book be a guide, a resource, and confirmation that you can achieve anything you set your mind, heart and soul to do. The women who contributed to this book have all had obstacles to overcome and failures along their way to success. They are ordinary women doing extraordinary things, and if they can achieve their dreams, you can too.

Please share it with a friend, send a copy to your mother, daughter, sister or colleague. The world needs more empowered women like you.

To your success,

Christine Kloser
www.NEWentrepreneurs.com

PART I

PERSONAL FULFILLMENT

CHAPTER 1

Discovering Motherhood and the Beauty of Letting Go

LOURDES BARDEN, MA

ELEVEN YEARS AGO, shortly around the time of my thirtieth birthday, my biological clock not only rang but exploded! It was time for marriage, time for a baby, and it seemed nothing would stop me. Think of me as the female version of the caveman finding his woman, hitting her over the head, and dragging her off to his cave. I would see a man, point, grunt and say, "You, you my husband! We make child!"

Just ask any of my long-time girlfriends and they'll tell you about Bruce, Richard, Alan, George, and a few others I can't remember and swear to this day I never thought of marrying. Of course, all of those relationships I tried to make happen in the hopes of fulfilling my biological destiny failed. Although my biological clock had rung, my spiritual and emotional clocks were far from ready for motherhood. At 30 it seemed I knew what motherhood was, what it should look like, and when and how I should do it. However, reality lay far beneath the surface, hidden by my own ideas and the morass of cultural messages I had unconsciously taken on.

FINDING MY WAY

My approach to discovering motherhood was to take classes and read every book possible on the subject. In truth, nothing can prepare us for motherhood except motherhood herself. The birth experience is an excellent example. No matter how many books you read or classes you take, nothing can prepare you for the reality of the birth experience. The gift of life is guided by an absolutely unforeseeable and uncontrollable force. All we can do is go with it, and motherhood is the same way.

So how do we discover motherhood and prepare for something we can't prepare for? The secret to the illusionary preparation is right under our nose: it is our life. We discover motherhood by learning to LET GO and practice this art through living our lives. We prepare by fearlessly moving toward what we believe in and find our way through what a close friend calls our "messes and redundancies."

MAKING A MESS OVER AND OVER AGAIN

I can honestly say I have spent a considerable amount of time making a mess of my life. I have also made the same mess in different ways on several occasions, each bearing its lessons and bringing me closer to understanding. As I mentioned previously, I tried to orchestrate the mysterious events of marriage and motherhood. Each relationship I attempted to cajole into existence failed—one all the way up to six months before the wedding day!

This particular event sent me on a crying binge for what seemed like a year. Grief, with its powerful and uncontrollable force, arrived to help me reconcile my life. I was deeply disappointed; God had slammed the door shut to my aspirations. I was being set straight like a two year old who wanted but could not have.

As I saw it, I really had no choice, and the only way out was through it. Standing at the well of grief looking down into its darkness, I chose to let go and jumped into its cool abyss. The tears came and washed away my pain, my sorrow, my hope, and every last bit of genius I had on how I thought my life should be. I let go and let it clean me out like the slow drizzle of sand in a five thousand hour hourglass.

In time, I faced the reality that I was different, and I would not follow the paths of my sisters, my mother, and the countless other women who were married and had their babies by 30. I let go of the vision that I would be like my weird Aunt Joan who died alone and barren and held out the hope there was something better for me, something I didn't know existed. Finally at the bottom of the well, my soul caught me and I realized that letting go as a lifestyle was the only way for me to be happy.

THE PRACTICE OF LETTING GO

Letting go is an art. In the beginning of the practice we often think when we first let go, our work is done. However, we soon find out we have to let go every single day for the rest of our lives. As a therapist put it to me one day while in the throws of what to do with my life and one of my potential fathers: "Don't pursue, don't withdraw, just be."

This brings me to my best story—my husband. I could not be luckier to have Eric in my life. It is by the grace of God that I found someone so genuine, kind, and loving because I never could have found him on my own. Of course he came into my life when I least expected it, and he didn't fit the image of my Prince Charming. But isn't that the point?

Life is sweeter when we say thank you and allow ourselves to be pleasantly surprised by what it has to offer, rather than forcing it to bend to our will. When asked how we got together, I share about the evening we were enjoying each other's company in a friend's living room. Looking at Eric, his face and heart so sweet with love, I thought: "Wow! This man loves me! If he has the guts to trust that love, we'll get married! AND I LET IT GO! As a matter of fact, I forgot about it and went on with my life, enjoyed dating him, and took it one day at a time. I didn't pursue or withdraw I just was.

SOMETIMES IT TAKES A CESAREAN, AMBULANCE RIDE, HURRICANE AND A FLOOD TO LET GO

My reaction to pregnancy at 40 was sheer joy. I was one of the lucky ones; I got pregnant the first month we tried. However, despite God's grace, I felt compelled to figure it out so I hit the books and started reading about what everyone had to say. Doing so sent me into a state of worry.

According to the medical professionals, a woman at my age could face a variety of complications such as fetal abnormalities, chromosomal defects, placenta previa, stillbirth, diabetes, and more. I felt angry and trapped by the statistics, and I began my battle of trying to determine what I would trust. I decided that if God planned for me to have a baby with a defect it was fine with me. I decided to trust the entire situation, embraced it positively, breathed in, and let go.

However, as time progressed my old friend "control" snuck up on me and started doing its work. When we are pregnant, we often-times do things that only have rhyme or reason to the pregnant woman herself. It just has to be done! A friend of mine painted everything in her home blue. She hated it after the baby was born, but it seemed to be a necessity while she was pregnant. Myself, I took to organizing, cleaning, and remodeling. There was not a towel, sock, or sheet out of place in our home. I painted, remodeled the bathroom, and put a new floor in the laundry room.

I got ready for the biggest mystery of my life by putting my external life in as much order as I possibly could. I paid every bill, stocked the cupboards, and tied up every loose end. Deep down I was scared of what lay ahead and order gave me solace. Despite my hopes that order would rock me through birth, Nourah's arrival was far from an orderly experience.

I was a new mom, naïve, and had developed a hopeful case of amnesia to the realities of Mother Nature. My husband and best friend said I was calm when I found out the baby was under fetal stress; calm that I would be taking an ambulance ride from my birth oasis complete with candles and music to the cold and sterile environment of the hospital. I knew what lay ahead; it was familiar territory.

Once again in life's beautiful way, I was being catapulted into the reality of what was and away from what I desired. It happens, and it was happening to me. I let go and gave birth to a new reality—the one happening in the here and now. Nourah and I made it through, and she came into the world healthy and by emergency c-section, but life had one more surprise.

We were home with Nourah for a week when Katrina brought three straight days of rain to Washington DC. I enjoyed the rain; I found it comforting, until I found about six inches of it on my bedroom floor! Before I knew it, our carpet was up, furniture moved all around, and huge fans blowing. The sanctuary I had built for my family was destroyed, the peace gone.

As I lay on our couch in a smelly wind tunnel, I took my pulse. I thought I might have a heart attack. I was like Sanford saying, "This is the big one!" So I breathed in, let go, and cried. In his infinite wisdom my loving husband said, "Everything will be all right honey." And of course, he was right!

LOURDES BARDEN MA, spiritual counselor and peak performance coach of 15 years, has worked with many individuals unique in their passions and interests. She is the founder of Mommy Coaches, a coaching service that supports mothers to create and live a unique vision of their lives as mother. Lourdes has led numerous workshops and one-day seminars for personal growth and self-empowerment. She was the original founder of Healing the Mother Wound and co-facilitator with Gordon Clay in the Family Reunion Workshops. Lourdesbarden@yahoo.com (202) 986-3430

CHAPTER 2

The Power of Volition!

MARIAN BATTS-TURNER, MSN, RN, CDE

I'M NOT GOING to share with you anything you don't know or haven't heard about the steps to achieve optimal health or personal success. However, I will share with you my epiphany revealing why success eluded me for so long despite my knowledge and quest.

I'm not speaking from my professional experience as a health care provider and research scientist seeking ways to improve the health of people with chronic diseases like diabetes for over a decade. My message comes straight from the heart and my personal journey to wellness!

My epiphany came one day (Sunday, June 5, 2005 to be exact) as I read yet another self-help book when suddenly I experienced déjà vu. It occurred to me that many of the books and articles I'd read shared the same fundamental messages—with all I'd read and experienced, I had all the knowledge needed to achieve my goals. So, why hadn't I achieved success? I counted dozens of books and countless articles read, now sitting on my bookshelf or neatly filed away for "future reference". And still success continued to elude me again and again. Have you ever felt as though you were glued in one spot no matter how hard you tried to move, wiggle, or shake yourself free to take a step? What was preventing me from taking the step from setting goals to accomplishing goals?

Numerous reasons came to mind—my favorite was: "I'm a single parent and work too hard which leaves little time to exercise, make healthy meal choices, or concentrate on completing my business plan". All of the reasons were simply symptoms of the real problem—lack of volition!

I was always confident I knew what to do and certain of how important it was to do it but somewhere deep within I was my own barrier—I lacked the will to make the difference for myself.

So often, we place others ahead of ourselves—their needs, desires, and goals. How can we focus on ourselves without feeling selfish or neglectful of those we care about and love? How can we take time away from our important work to make ourselves a priority? Before my epiphany, my answer was "as soon as *this* was done or *that* project was complete or so & so had what they needed from me". Now my answer has become "how can I not show myself the same love and respect I give to others? How can I be of any value to others if I don't value myself?"

My "new" attitude didn't happen overnight but has and continues to be a daily—even minute by minute—process of reconnecting with the woman in the mirror through Positive Self-Talk!

Discover and embrace the art of Positive Self-Talk—communicating with yourself from within in a loving and affirming way! This isn't rocket science or a patented system only available to those with a VISA. It's not a hard concept to understand since most of us have mastered the art of Negative Self-Talk. However, it isn't an easy concept to implement.

POSITIVE SELF-TALK TO ACHIEVE PERSONAL SUCCESS

There are many ways we can think and talk ourselves out of doing what's best for us or reaching for our goals. BUT, there are even more powerful ways we can think and talk ourselves into and through a process of transformation!

LAYING THE FOUNDATION

It's okay to focus on me. Unless you get that fundamental concept and keep it at the forefront of your thoughts, you'll only have negative self-talk to rely on. A great way to remind you is to choose a mantra (your personal mission statement or thoughts about you). Write it down! Place it in your line of vision at home, work, etc. Recite it every morning upon rising and evening before going to bed. While it might seem hokey at first, trust that it works!

I'm responsible for my own success. Me and me alone.
Each failure is one step closer to success.
I owe it to myself to be successful!

SETTING THE GOAL

Where do you want to be? Seriously consider what that will look like. Visualize what the end looks like. Perhaps you see yourself physically fit or nourishing a thriving business or both. Whatever it is, take a picture and archive it. Again, write it down! Seriously, whether it's a drawing of that perfect body or simply a written description of the type of business you want, it's important to document your dream. Make a commitment to remind yourself daily!

I want to be healthy & happy—ALIVE & weighing 145

CREATING THE PLAN

How do you plan to get there? Start out by being realistic. Plan to do one step at a time. Choose P over P—progress not perfection —to combat any negative self-talk along the way! We're comfortable documenting our accomplishments on resumes, applications, surveys, etc.: however, the idea of writing down our dreams and goals can be frightening to many, especially when the benefits of going after them never seem to outweigh the costs. Creating a "life plan" is crucial to achieving success. You have a vision but what will be the path from here to there. We're all familiar with the adage if you fail to plan then you plan to fail. How true it is! Your mantra and goal are actually the beginning of your life plan. The next step is to break down your global goal(s) into smaller, achievable steps. Granted you want to lose 60 lbs. or earn a six-figure income. But, you won't achieve either of these goals just by setting them. There has to be a strategy for getting there. Perhaps the first step is losing 5 pounds monthly until you're looking like a million dollars. Embracing P over P will never leave you feeling defeated!

Lose 5 pounds this month.
- Get up and move at least 20 minutes daily.
- Drink at least 8 glasses of water daily.
Even if I don't lose the 5 pounds, I'm bound to
accomplish something when I focus on the smaller steps.

STAYING ON TRACK

Getting there won't happen overnight. Life's a journey—a continuum not a finite set of achievements. No one's perfect and everyone will fall off track at some point. However, when the focus is the journey toward the goal and not the goal, staying the course is more palpable. You've got to have checkpoints along the way (review your "life plan"). It's not smart to invest in setting goals and making plans to reach them if we don't commit to checking up on ourselves. At times it might be painful, especially if we've had a bump in the road. But, we can only recover and resume the plan when we evaluate. What do we do when we only lose 4 of those 5 pounds?! We repeat our mantra, revisit our vision, and choose P over P!

Lost 3 lbs. this month!
- *Walked 15 minutes daily.*
- *Started Karate classes with my son.*
- *Up to 10 glasses of water daily.*

I've made progress!!!

CELEBRATING

What will happen once you arrive? It's going to take time; something novel in the society we've come to know where everything is instantaneous! But, if you make a plan and work the plan, you'll reach your goal. It's the law of nature, the world is round and what you put out comes back to you! Investing in positive self-talk guarantees positive results! Maybe not in your desired time but definitely when due. Deciding what you'll do when you accomplish each of your achievable steps on the way to your ultimate goal is an important responsibility. Celebrating each achievement is a form of positive self-talk ("Look what I've accomplished and I'm celebrating me!") and actually magnifies the effect of positive self-talk!

My first manicure and pedicure in too long. (I'm hooked!)
More achievements = more dates at the day spa!

What has positive self-talk done for me? My mantra starts, ends and journeys with me through each day. My vision for the future is clear and becomes more vivid and real with each celebration. My plan is alive (a work in progress, not stagnant or collecting dust). I cherish my celebrations and work hard to keep my dates with my manicurist and (now) masseuse! There's less stress and while I didn't logically see how I could achieve my goal to weigh 145 lbs.— I've actually surpassed that goal. I'm doing things in Karate I'd never thought possible—I'm a Purple belt! A new goal is to go all the way and earn a Black belt (a ridiculously, wonderful goal to me). I'm also stepping out on faith and working on my business versus on my business plan. I'm committed to helping others embrace the art of positive self-talk and create the lives they want for themselves through Real Matters Consulting, LLC. Workshops, individual counseling sessions, and support groups are all avenues we employ to help our clients.

MARIAN has an MSN in Advanced Practice Nursing from Johns Hopkins University; with faculty appointments in Medicine and Nursing. Marian's expertise includes disease management; clinician & patient communication; self-discovery & personal transformation; program development & evaluation; and grant writing. She's presented nationally and published in peer-reviewed journals. Contact Real Matters Consulting LLC at (410) 608-5198, nursemlb@msn.com, or 6400 Baltimore National Pike, Suite 344, Catonsville, MD 21228. Visit www.realmattersnow.com for a free newsletter subscription.

CHAPTER 3

A Woman's Guide to Transforming Patterns of Anger & Stress into Personal Power & Success

ANUTZA BELLISSIMO, CAMF

ANGER IN THE AIR

AS A DESCENDANT from a long line of angry women, I found within myself the need to break the chains of bondage that have plagued the women in my family for so many decades. It is my intention to share how I have transformed my personal relationships, business struggles, and parenting skills in order to exemplify various patterns of anger that have hindered my self-empowerment. It is known, that the first eight years of development mold a child's future as an adult. Whether those years are nurturing or lacking emotional bonds, anger reveals itself more than any other emotion. Anger is one of the most misunderstood and overused human emotions; henceforth anger is a signal.

A beginning everyone is familiar with, for better or worse, is childhood. The few memories I can recall as an innocent child were of my mother, replacing love for me with anger. Her hurtful communication burned my social bridges as a growing child in need of my mother's love and acceptance. Sadly, the only time I felt warmth from her was after it left a welted sting. My experiences as an adolescent were not any more communicative, lacking the motherly lessons a growing teenager depends on in order to gain respect and confidence in one's self.

As an adolescent, my experiences intensified my doubts and shortcomings as a child. I remember wanting to understand why situations in my life happened the way they did. Throughout my life, I felt abandoned, confused, alone and resentful due to my fear of communicating authentically with others. My mother's manipulation over control and power left me feeling unworthy of love and attention. As a child, I had undergone many forms of abuse inflicted by people I trusted.

I grew to believe that women were incapable of unconditional love and acceptance. The next 20 years of my life were spent struggling with fears of inadequacy. I was consumed by my attempts to relieve painful remnants of self doubt; I desperately felt the need to reinvent myself. It was especially challenging to reevaluate my experiences when so much of my adult life referred back to my interpretations as a child. Nonetheless, I realized my life was the result of the choices I had made.

THE POSSIBILITY OF INSPIRING LEADERSHIP

My intention is to inspire empowering paths of self motivation by expressing to others my journey and zest for life. At the age of 19, without proper business training, I set out to be the proud owner of a nail and skin salon. I found myself challenged by the everyday responsibilities of being an established entrepreneur: interviewing, managing, inventory, marketing, etc. I was young, nervous and inexperienced, but I had the drive and courage to take a chance.

My business survived almost a year. I closed the salon due to lack of clientele and capital. I recall walking away feeling ashamed and hopeless. It brought me back to my childhood feelings of not being good enough. In looking back on it, I believe it was my lack of self esteem and faith that prohibited my progress in building my business.

After numerous business endeavors, I came to discover Life Purpose Coaching. Launching a new and successful business to aid others as a Life Purpose Coach, my career involved proven and motivational methods for women in need of redirection. This practice gave me the opportunity to honestly contribute to the lives of individuals. Powerfully and successfully, I used my intuition in helping guide clients to a happy and healthy life of self expression.

As a professional speaker in the Life Purpose/Career Coaching arena, I catered to audiences that had been laid off/"down sized" or individuals who were desperately seeking new ways of reinventing themselves. I knew firsthand what it would take to change and reinvent one's self after loss, business failure, abusive relationships or even sexual abuse. Realizing I could relate and contribute, I began working with others and noticed my hostility beginning to dissipate. The rage I carried within myself no longer served my purpose.

My career as a "Life Purpose Coach" evolved into stress and anger management facilitation for the State of California at the Stress & Anger Management Institute (S.A.M.I.). I specialize in educating women how to manage stress and anger in the workplace, as parents, and in personal relationships. One can achieve positive communication levels by clearly eliminating *inattention* or *avoidance* as a response to fear and anxiety. By providing simple strategies that implement educational tools, I teach how to recognize patterns of *resentment* and *control* that prevent us from living life to its fullest.

I'd like to share the story of a young woman who at the age of 22 was in desperate need of stress and anger management tools. Struggling with a co-dependent relationship, she had found the assertiveness to make changes in her life, yet she needed guidance to coach her along the hardest phase of change. She called one day in need of counsel and comfort. I asked, "Heather, is everything okay?"

She replied through choked tears, "No, this move is really painful for me. I feel like my world is falling apart!" In order to help her breathing slow down, I said, "Don't let the negativity around you get the better of this situation, breath in…breath out…everything is happening the way it should."

My heart went out to her. Heather confided, " I … am … so … angry. My … stomach is in knots … I … feel … sick … with … anxiety." Heather was experiencing extreme levels of *conflict*, *hopelessness* and *guilt* due to the situation at hand.

I coached her by saying, "Heather, repeat after me. Everything is okay. Say it with me… Everything is okay. These are only life lessons you must learn from. Relationship failure does not make you a bad person; everything is happening the way it should."

After a few short moments, she regulated her breathing and continued to make her move. Through redirection of mind and heart, her confidence resurfaced in order to aid her in better decision making.

As a parent, I have learned the importance of genuinely *expressing feelings* through sharing *honest feedback* in a loving and *assertive* manner. The importance of *seeking compromise* in parenting relationships and *focusing* on positive outcomes is pivotal to living an inspiring life. Teaching children to "listen to the voice inside" and express their needs, whether large or small, is a primary factor in the health and vitality of body and soul. Empowerment can be found in *active listening*, by allowing children the opportunity to rephrase negative thoughts and feelings. This exercise alone will strengthen the bond between parent and child by expressively creating positive energy.

Anger management is a work of motivational interviewing and

personal healing. By gaining a clear understanding of self, we can learn to better control our anger so it does not lead to violent outbursts or actions that are harmful to others. Learning different techniques to manage stress, enhance emotional intelligence and improve communication encourages better listening and communication skills. This will help prevent stressful or angry situations.

In November of 2005, I proudly introduced a new and very important aspect of my practice, the "S.A.M.I. Pillow.®" I invented this interactive communication tool in order to help adults and adolescents learn to master communication skills, emotional intelligence, self-esteem as well as stress and anger management skills. The pillow's main function is to serve adults and adolescents as an anchor in stress and anger management education, with a simple flip of the pillow, the embroidered language teaches how to transform negative interaction into positive interaction with others or within the individual (self-talk).

For example; a parent and adolescent relationship would benefit by using this tool to learn better ways of communicating, by simply identifying with the S.A.M.I. Pillows negative interactions in their behavior and replacing them with the suggested positive interactions on the pillow. The language on the pillow, such as, over-reacting vs. self-correcting and suppression vs. expression are some examples. The same process could be used in a workplace environment or individual setting.

Whether it's used in the workplace, parenting or couple relationships, the S.A.M.I. Pillow is an excellent educational tool for those interested in improving their communication, stress, or anger management skills.

There are many things you can do to prevent stress from escalating into anger. By simply identifying negative emotions/action such as denial, anxiety, conflict, hopelessness, suppression, shame, guilt or over-reacting, we can change the pattern of negative behavior into positive emotions/action such as acceptance, clarity, enthusiasm, expression, forgiveness, self-worth, generous listening and self-correcting.

On www.KLASFM.com, "S.A.M.I. Radio", I teach how to learn acceptable expressions of anger, manage stress accordingly, how to eliminate self-destructive patterns from our lives and how to implement the S.A.M.I. Pillow. I encourage anyone interested in transforming patterns of anger and stress into personal power and success to contact me for more information about the Stress and Anger Management Institute or the S.A.M.I. Pillow. I wish you all the best life has to offer.

ANUTZA BELLISSIMO, CAMF is the founder of the Stress & Anger Management Institute; Anutza is a certified Adult and Adolescent Anger Management Facilitator providing individual executive coaching, group classes, employee training, workshops, and seminars, specializing in psycho-education; teaching skills in managing stress, anger, improving communication and enhancing emotional intelligence in the workplace, couple relationships and parenting. For more information contact the Stress & Anger Management Institute at www.abcamf.com or call (310) 545-8767.

CHAPTER 4

Refocus, Reframe & Take Risks
The Mantra for Success

KIM R. MORGAN, PH.D.
& MARSHA CATON-FAUSTIN, PH.D.

HAVE YOU EVER WONDERED about the origin of popular child-hood games? Were these games a product of a child's imagination or were they created by adults in order to teach children valuable lessons about life?

I remember one particular childhood game that was very popular when I was growing up. It was called *freeze-tag*. In this game, children attempt to tag each other and the unfortunate "frozen" child must stop all movement until another teammate saves the frozen player by re-tagging, and thus 'un-freezing', him/her.

I strongly believe that the overarching tenets of this childhood game teach very important lessons to both children and adults alike. You may ask, what are these important lessons? The lessons include learning how to evaluate your situation, set goals, develop an action plan, and whole-heartily pursue your ambitions.

Have you ever told yourself, "I'm not good enough," or "I really want to get ahead but it's too hard?" Or, have you ever offered the popular lamentation of, "I really want to do it, but I can't because of my age / economic status / color / weight / children / job /

responsibilities?" If you have used any variation of these excuses, then you, my friend, are in essence playing freeze-tag as an adult. However, this version of the game is no longer on the playground with friends. Instead, it's in your mind.

Although the concept is very similar, playing freeze-tag as an adult, in our own minds, has a different set of rules. In this version of the game, we, as adults, have the ability to both freeze and un-freeze ourselves. Freezing ourselves means that we enter a state of inertia. In this state, we know what we want to accomplish but we refuse to move forward because we fear imminent failure. In the frozen state, it is not uncommon for us to rationalize our excuses and think very little of our God-given talents and capabilities. Unfortunately, this type of negative thinking causes us to stay in a perpetual frozen state, afraid of attempting anything that is outside of the normal routine or realm of reality.

How do we unfreeze ourselves once we are in a frozen state? Successful businesses and people, for that matter, always have a clear and defined plan and so should you! Without exception, the first step to success is to clearly define your ultimate goals. Ask yourself, "What motivates me?" and "What am I most passionate about?" Perform a SWOT analysis—a breakdown of Strengths, Weaknesses, Opportunities and Threats. After reviewing your self-analysis, write down your immediate (less than 1 year), short-term (within 1- 5 years) and long-term (5 years or more) goals. Post them in an area where you will see them often. Remember, your plan need not be perfect, but it must be specific and clearly defined. Make sure to avoid becoming frozen again by playing the game in real-time; in other words, be present in the moment. Put your plans into action and make adjustments as you go along.

Once you have clear and defined goals, reframe your outlook on your situation. Reframing involves redefining your context and changing your outlook on a given situation. Change all negative internal dialogs by replacing negative words with positive affirmations. Visualize yourself as the person you want to become. Do not focus on why you do not want to stay in your current situation because this encourages a negative outlook. Instead, focus on challenging your mind to generate new ideas and approaches in order to achieve your goal. For example, instead of saying, "I can't," think of ways in which you can accomplish your goals.

Increase your knowledge base by involving others in your journey. Find a mentor, read books, and search the internet to find helpful suggestions and motivational stories. Surround yourself with people who have positive attitudes. Join groups dedicated to your cause. Refocus your energies to support a defined set of goals! Reframe negative thoughts with positive affirmations! And above all else, garnish the courage to take risks in order to win the game and ultimately have free reign over your life!

The Courage to Take Risks:

Why Risk-taking Need not be
so Precarious...

MARSHA CATON-FAUSTIN, PH.D.

WHY ARE YOU AFRAID to take risks? Why do you walk away from countless opportunities because of uncertainties? You must ask yourself these questions and answer them honestly from your heart. Proverbs 23:7 states, "As a man thinks in his heart, so is he." This proverbial attitude is the foundation of any successful individual's mindset. That is to say, if you wholeheartedly believe that goals and dreams are attainable, then they are; it is just that simple. Of course, the opposite is also true. If you truly believe that you cannot achieve your goals, then by default, you will not attain them.

Understanding this tenet of the "law of success" is only one of the essential cornerstones of building an accomplished life. The foundation, walls, floors, and ceilings of successful life-construction, lie in a variety of factors, which include strategic planning, clear goal definition, and knowing when to take risks.

It is accurate to think of risk taking as the plumb-line of one's success, since the breadth of your success is determined by the breadth of your risk. The term 'risk taking' is not meant to infer that we engage in frivolous hand waving, while abandoning intuition and throwing all caution to the wind in the face of obvious danger. I believe risk taking can be an informed decision. There may be no clear indication of the end result, but there will always be indications of whether the beginning and/or the middle hold any significant promise at all. In such a circumstance, the odds should be considered, after which one can decide to take a leap of faith, while trusting that hard work and perseverance will culminate in a successful end product.

Undoubtedly, taking risks, informed or otherwise, requires courage. Yet, there is one caveat; I have found that the most expedient courage required for success is the courage to take an introspective gaze. The courage to face our own shortcomings and limitations is true courage. Anyone can look outward and delineate problematic situations, but how many truly dare to look inward?

An earnest introspective look often deposits a sense of powerlessness into our mental and emotional accounts. Why so? Unfeigned honesty forces us to resuscitate our consciousness that we are not self-sufficient. This realization forces us to peaceably reconcile with the notion that our fate does not depend solely on us, but that we need others in order to truly be successful.

Is there a mogul in today's society that does not depend on the subscription of the public sector for success? We can mention many names, but all of these success models rely on others to execute their operations. So what's the point you may ask? The admonition is simply that the model for life is one of interdependence; we are designed to need others. We should not retreat from allowing ourselves to live in the fullness of our inter-dependence, especially as we strive towards our life fulfillment.

Now that we have unearthed our vulnerability, what do we do with it? We capitalize on such a great opportunity! By this I mean we take the thing that makes us most vulnerable, and we conquer it! Yes, we need people, but people also need us. Having accepted this knowledge, we have gained ground on which we can measure out the steps needed to be successful. The goal, once we acknowledge and embrace our inter-dependence, is to develop the excellence of character and skill that guarantees our success. If one sows excellence, one reaps excellence; if slothfulness, one reaps slothfulness. This principle holds true regardless of our faith, or lack thereof. It is demonstrated in nature and the same holds true in other areas of life. We reap what we sow.

The take-home principle is simply to make yourself an asset to those around you, regardless of the arena you operate in. If you are building a business, make your product or service one that your target customer must have, market excellence. In your home, create an atmosphere of excellence and watch the generational benefits of your seed. The ultimate realization on the road to success is that once cultivated in the way of true excellence, your gifts will pave the way for you.

Once you define your plans, refocus and reframe your energies and take the risk of honest self assessment, attaining your goals and realizing your dreams will be a rewarding journey. Undoubtedly, there will be challenges and struggles along the way, but with a focused mind and heart, all obstacles will be surmounted. Lastly, while on the exhilarating road to success, embrace others and be inter-dependent. This makes your load infinitely lighter and will free you to enjoy your success as you build it.

KIM R. MORGAN, PH.D., is a Regulatory Scientist and the founder and president of Accelerated Achievements, LLC, an educational services company (www.acceleratedachievements.com). Dr. Morgan can be contacted at drkim@acceleratedachievements.com. Marsha Caton-Faustin, Ph.D., is a Molecular Geneticist and co-founder of TriState Reclaim Medical Management, LLC, a full service Medical Group Management Company, headquartered in Burtonsville, Maryland (www.trimmclaims.com). Dr. Caton-Faustin can be contacted at drcatonfaustin@trimmclaims.com. Dr. Morgan and Caton-Faustin are also motivational coaches.

CHAPTER 5

⌒

Healing Yourself With Music
PEGGY JAEGLY

THE WESTERN WORLD recently rediscovered what ancient Greeks have known: music can be used to heal and change the state of a person's being. Healing means that a person can experience increased comfort in the present moment, as opposed to curing, which is the eradication of disease or malfunction.

A simple recipe for using music will enhance your life. The sentence, "**Music I.S. R.E.S.T.**" will help you remember all the ingredients. The acronym stands for: **I**ntention, **S**ilence, **R**esonant Tone, **E**ntrainment, **S**ound Bath, and **T**empo.

INTENTION

Before beginning, it is important to set your intention. Do you need to be energized? Do you desire to feel more settled? Do you want to spark your creativity?

Scientist Don Estes, author of *Harmonic Law: The Science of Vibration*, states that "Because the harp has no frets, i.e. the strings don't hit against something when played, the vibrations produced by the harp strings go on forever." So when I play for a patient, my musical meditations and songs are accompanied by my intentions for peace and healing. These offerings then, by the nature of the harp, are a perpetual intention for the patient.

Even more important than the music played is the intention. Decide first, what do you want to create for yourself?

SILENCE

Throughout the day, sounds bombard us. Do you go through your day with the radio playing, the television turned on to keep you company, and your computer running to beep for each incoming email? Do telephone calls, doorbells and buzzers interrupt your day? I would encourage you to first experience silence.

If you sometimes feel off kilter, somewhat unhappy, or depressed, turning off the sounds and walking or sitting in silence will allow true problems to surface. Five of the most healing days I ever spent were on a solo silent retreat at a monastery set in a mountain far from home. There was no television, radio, or music allowed. The phones were locked, preventing both incoming and outgoing phone calls. Speech was not permitted, even with other patrons visiting in the same house. I went to meditate and pray on the direction of my life and that of my family. Initially, I thought one particular challenge had brought me to a crossroad. But instead, the silence permitted the true and unexpected issue of my discontent to rise to the surface like cream rises to the top of a milk bottle.

Once you have experienced silence, gently reintroduce sound. Keep in mind that preferences for music are individual. As a working mother of three, my music preferences tend toward the very soft and soothing songs as a counterpoint to my demanding life. My son, on the other hand, preferred rap, one of my least favorite genres of music. He worked hard to overcome dyslexia, a condition in which the processes of the brain mix the appearance of letters and words. I realized that pattern was what was absent from his life and he seemed to seek that in his music selections.

Experiment to determine your best balance between silence and sound. In my work, sometimes the space between the notes, in addition to the music played, is a vital tool to healing.

RESONANT TONE

Everyone has what is called a resonant tone. A resonant tone is a particular note that when it is played, causes your whole body to resonate at the same vibrational level and you feel wonderful. There are several ways to discover your resonant tone. One method I use is to have a person sit in an all-wooden chair. I lean my harp against the back of the chair and play one string at a time and ask for feedback from the person. There will be one particular note that seems to massage the person into a state of well-being.

If you suffer from daily irritations, and we all do, I find it helpful to think of people, especially those whose behavior irritates me, as "a different note." We need all the notes to make a song in our world. We all belong. If you tend to be too hard on yourself, remember that you are a special note, and the world needs you too. You have a purpose and add to life's symphony.

ENTRAINMENT

Healing musicians use something called entrainment. We meet the person musically at their current state, and then gradually, we move the music a bit at a time, closer to the intention for the person.

Where do you start when you want to introduce music into your day? Ask yourself how you are feeling. If you are feeling joyous, then you won't want to start with a lament. If you are feeling depressed, you don't want to start with an overly zealous song. The gap would be jarring. A slow transition from where you are to where you want to be will move you in the direction of your intention.

The ancient Greeks used modal music. Pythagoras, the father of music therapy, realized that certain keys of music created different states in people. Space limitations only permit me to mention a few examples. If you are feeling restless, you will want to listen to music that is grounding and has a strong bass sound. An example would be *Scarborough Fair,* which is based on the note D. If you want to feel happier, reminisce good memories, or calm a baby, listen to songs based around the note of C. Many of our childhood songs and lullabies are written in this key. If you want to alleviate pain, songs based around the note of A, for example, *Greensleeves,* will help you.

SOUND BATH

We love to pamper ourselves with bubble baths, manicures and pedicures but I consider it equally important to give yourself a sound bath. Pay attention to the sounds around you and how each one makes you feel. Sometimes we live and work in environments that have grating sounds to which we've blocked our awareness, but the cells in our bodies absorb that sound.

Our bodies are like a living musical instrument. In vibrational medicine, each part of the spine responds to a certain note of the scale. Each part of the spine protects nerves that serve various organs, which can also respond to music. UCLA recently published a study that indicated that the cells, which are precursors to developed heart cells, still pulsate when placed in a petri dish. When those pulses were recorded and amplified to the level of human hearing, they discovered the cells were "singing" a song similar to the song of whales.

Many scientific studies have concluded that music can lower blood pressure, increase oxygenation, regulate heartbeats, reduce pain, evoke good memories, and reduce stress. Make changes where possible to create the sounds that make you feel more energetic, creative and healthier.

For instance, I set the intention that I wanted my home to feel like a sanctuary for whoever enters it, including me. I keep the television and radio off. Instead, I play CDs of harp music, Indian flute or other soothing instruments in the background. My pet birds love the music just as much as I do and sing to their favorite CDs, adding to the feeling of a natural sanctuary where everyone is welcome and can rejuvenate.

TEMPO

Your preference for the pace of music will vary from day to day and be influenced by your current task. If you're cleaning house or exercising, you might prefer music with a strong beat and a faster pace. If you are eating dinner or writing a letter, you may prefer softer songs with a slower tempo. The choice is yours.

Our hearing develops while we are still in the womb starting when the fetus is about four months old. It is also one of the last senses we lose. I invite you to listen, experiment and discover the sounds and tempos that suit you the best. Manage the sounds around you as carefully as you pick an outfit to wear. Increasing your awareness of sounds and incorporating music in your daily life will help you soothe your inner spirit and create a state of mind that is most conducive to you manifesting your intentions.

PEGGY JAEGLY, CMP, HCMBH, CHM is a speaker, composer, Certified Music Practitioner, a Hospital Certified Master Bedside Harpist, Certified Healing Musician and owns her private practice of The Healing Harp and The Elegant Harp. Her life's mission is to promote peace and healing. She welcomes comments and questions at her email, peggy@peggyjaegly.com. For more information on her speaker and harp services, books and CDs call her at (410) 758-0059 or visit her website www.peggyjaegly.com.

CHAPTER 6

The Freedom Formula™

CHRISTINE KLOSER

DIFFERENT PEOPLE ASSOCIATE different meanings with the word "freedom," yet it's a common desire for all human beings. Everyone has a picture in their mind when they think of being free. To me, freedom is a universal quality of our human nature. It's something within you that's part of your Divine being. It was birthed in you the moment you were born. Your experience of freedom increases with your ability to operate from a place of inner peace and self-love. The clutter of your busy life, and the speed at which life happens can deprive you of experiencing freedom.

Having a sense of freedom is probably at the top of your values list. So, what does it really mean for you to be free?

For some people, freedom is where all things are possible. It's when the abundant flow of life magically unfolds in front of you, everyday. It may mean choosing what you want to do, and when you want to do it. It's about making choices in each moment based on your desire for freedom. For others it's when everything "clicks" and even the curveballs that come your way make sense. Perhaps it's when you know you are co-creating your life and have the power to manifest your heart's desire. It's when everything flows, when you're "in the zone."

This all sounds good, doesn't it? Isn't this how you want to live your life? In a way that feels easy, graceful, fulfilling, guided, relaxed, abundant, and stress-free. I feel a greater sense of freedom just writing those words. Imagine what it would be like to live in freedom all the time! I trust you can recall numerous moments when you felt absolutely free. One of my greatest "freedom" moments was standing under an archway of roses in Lake Arrowhead, California, on the most perfect sunny day imaginable… marrying my husband. I literally felt as if I was floating on air. Everything was fluid, my cheeks hurt from smiling so much, and I felt completely at ease and blessed. My wedding couldn't have been more perfect. I felt completely free on a day that I hear many women say was the most stressful day of their lives.

I made the decision to enjoy my wedding day and wanted to experience true freedom from the moment I woke up that day. I knew planning well in advance would help me experience freedom, as well as focusing on the moment without being wrapped up in the past or in the future. I was free because I made a conscious choice to act/be in a way that caused me to feel free. But, let's face it. Living like this everyday is impossible. Or, is it?

This is the question that brought me to developing The Freedom Formula™. You see, I'm the type of woman who wants it all, and I believe it's possible for me to have it all. I believe it's possible for you, too. Freedom is a state of mind within your reach at all times. In case your "monkey mind" is telling you it's not possible for you, remember that Nelson Mandela considered himself a free man, even when he was imprisoned. If he can be free in prison, you can experience freedom anywhere. But, how? By applying The Freedom Formula™.

I don't know about you, but I'm a "to do" list junkie. I'm the type that writes things on my list after they've already been done, just so

I can check them off the list. I know it's a bit crazy. But, for someone like me who wants to "do" everything and has to put conscious thought into "being," I wanted a formula. I wanted a concrete way to make the intangible, tangible.

What follows are the three steps of The Freedom Formula™. The formula can be applied to everything in your life. That is, any experience that leads to a feeling of lost freedom. Yes, any time you're doing something you don't want to do, or feel you "should" do something instead of what you're doing, or you feel trapped in indecision and don't know what choice to make… this formula will guide you through it all.

Using the following formula, you'll be considering every aspect of your life in which you don't feel completely free. This process will take some time to work through, but the good news is you can also apply The Freedom Formula ™ to experiences that arise in your everyday life. So, let's get started.

STEP I: ASSESS

In step one of The Freedom Formula™ you'll do an assessment. This is your opportunity to clearly identify what you believe deprives you of freedom. Before you begin any journey, you've got to know where you are, in order to help you identify where you want to go.

Begin your assessment by writing down everything that stops you from feeling a sense of freedom. Take your time to do a complete assessment. This is the foundation of the remaining two steps and the basis for applying The Freedom Formula™ in every area of your life. What you discover will set you on a firm path to true freedom.

As with any personal work like this, it may get uncomfortable for a while. You might experience anger, sadness, despair, or over-whelm. You might also experience relief, hope, clarity, or joy at the thought of experiencing more freedom in your life.

Here are a few things to think about to help you start your list. What keeps you from feeling freedom in relation to your:

- Health
- Marriage/Romantic Relationships
- Friendships
- Finances
- Family
- Parenting
- Business/Work
- Recreation
- Spirituality
- Sensuality
- Community
- Home/Environment
- Communication
- Creativity
- Thoughts

Next, choose one area to focus on as you go through the remaining two steps of The Freedom Formula™. The one to focus on first is the one that feels like it would bring you the most freedom when it's resolved.

STEP II: ASK

Now that you have a particular area of focus, ask for guidance from your higher power, Source, Spirit, God (whatever you call the force that makes trees bloom after a cold, dark winter). There are many different ways you can ask to be guided. Here are a few suggestions to start:

1. Journaling—Write the question you'd like to receive guidance about on a blank page in your journal. (ie. What would help me

release the lack of freedom I feel about my weight?) After you write the question, begin writing the answer. If you don't know what to write, begin by writing "I don't know what to write." Once the pen starts moving, and you keep focusing on the question, guidance will follow.

2. Sitting Meditation—Find a quiet space to sit in silence. Focus on your breath and allow yourself to become still. Imagine the top of your head opening to receive a beam of white light and ask for guidance on what would bring freedom to you in the area of _____. Continue focusing on the question and remain open to receiving your guidance. The message may come to you as a physical sensation, a hunch, smile, audible words, picture, or overall "Aha" feeling.

3. Conscious Awareness—Rather than sitting down to write or meditate, simply bring your question into awareness by asking it just as you would in the sitting meditation. You can do this while you're showering, doing dishes, gardening, taking a walk, or any activity that allows your mind to focus on something other than the task at hand.

In the sitting meditation and conscious awareness exercise, you may also want to write down your guidance soon after you receive it. This will help anchor your insights so you can move on to step three easily.

In the retreats I lead, I hear "thank you" after "thank you" from participants for giving them the space to ask for guidance. It seems so simple, yet it's something many people aren't in the habit of practicing.

STEP III: ACT

This is where The Freedom Formula™ becomes tangible, and very powerful. In step three, you will take a course of action based on the guidance you received in step two. Action is based in conscious choice, which is your key to freedom, and available at any moment.

For example, while I was writing this chapter, I took a break for dinner. When I left the kitchen to get back to writing, my 14 month old daughter made it known she preferred that I stay with her. Without applying The Freedom Formula™ I would have unconsciously stopped walking to my computer, turned around to be with her and then resented that I couldn't get back to writing. I was experiencing a great flow in my writing and wanted to maintain that momentum.

Instead, I applied The Freedom Formula™ by literally stopping on the landing of the stairs to acknowledge I was feeling a lack of freedom as it related to being a mother. I felt I was the only one who could console her and that I had to go to her. Next, I asked for guidance through Conscious Awareness and remained open to receive guidance. It said to pause a few more moments to see if she really needed me, or I just thought she needed me. What do you think happened? While I was being guided to pause, she quickly stopped being vocal and went to listen to my husband playing his guitar. Then, I made the conscious choice to hop on my computer to write.

I share this story because it demonstrates a simple "in the moment" application of The Freedom Formula™. When you are willing to Assess, Ask, and Act, the power of The Freedom Formula™ works every time. Imagine how good it will feel when you move through feelings of lost freedom instantaneously. The more you use this technique, the more quickly you'll receive guidance, and the more confidently you will act by making conscious choices.

Now, if you'll excuse me, I hear my daughter giggling in the bathtub and after acknowledging I'm not feeling a sense of freedom right now, I'm being guided to make the choice to go be with her!

CHRISTINE KLOSER, President of Love Your Life Publishing, Founder of NEW Entrepreneurs, Inc., Author of the **Inspiration to Realization** *book series and Mom of Janet Rose, has been an entrepreneur since 1991. She educates, inspires and empowers thousands of women entrepreneurs through ezines, retreats, work-shops, coaching programs, keynotes, and books. She's received widespread media attention including* **Entrepreneur Magazine,** **Making It TV,** **Los Angeles Times** *and* **Woman's Day.** *Learn how to fulfill your business, spiritual and personal dreams by subscribing to her FREE New Connections ezine: www.NEWnewsletter.com. publish@NEWentrepreneurs.com*

CHAPTER 7

Infinite Possibilities:
Five Steps to Identify
and Realize Your Dreams
ALEXIS MARTIN, ESQ.

I ONCE BELIEVED that being successful meant being a doctor or a lawyer or a manager. I had no idea that my career could be something I created and that I was limited only by my own imagination. Though my father was a business owner and I loved him immensely, I never aspired to own a business because my father's line of business embarrassed me. My dad sold business opportunities and through watching him I learned, or so I thought, that an educated person with common sense didn't aspire to own a business—educated people got real jobs. Daily, I thank the Universe that early in my career I discovered my misconceptions were keeping me in a job that would never allow me to really live my dreams. Business is indeed in my blood, AND there is nothing better than being a business owner! Today, I am free of the misinformation of my childhood and have the joy of realizing my own infinite possibilities.

My career first began at a prestigious law firm. As soon as I got to The Firm, I felt as though I was done—I had achieved my goals and now I could spend the rest of my life enjoying the fruits of my labor! Guess what? I was only 27! Quickly, the restlessness settled in; was this all life had to offer? Was this all life was about? A steady paycheck (almost half of which was gone to taxes) and no control over my own destiny? Was I forever condemned to answering to someone else and doing things their way? I began to think I had made a big mistake. At first I blamed myself; maybe there was something wrong with me since I could not appreciate this amazing job. Maybe I should never have gone to law school. Maybe if I could just fit in better with the other attorneys at The Firm, I would be happier. Thankfully, a confluence of events occurred around the same time that allowed me to see the Truth (no, you are not imagining it, that is Truth with a capital T).

The Truth was that there was nothing wrong with me! Yes, I am unique and being unique is wonderful and amazing, not something to be ashamed of. I was merely limited in my thinking. If I could tap into the limitless possibilities that are open to each of us, I could be and do and have everything I ever wanted. So, you ask, what in the heck does that really mean? Well, let me take you back to the way the Universe pointed me in the right direction. And that is **Step One in Identifying and Realizing Your Dreams: Follow the Signs!** Pay attention to the signs that show up in your life and take action whenever you see one.

First, I was "hired" by one of the partners of the law firm to prepare his family's estate plan. This partner was known to be particularly demanding. For example, he called me at 10 am on a Sunday, which happened to be my birthday, to discuss his planning, and he saw no reason that I shouldn't stop my preparations and talk with him right then when he called! I was quite nervous to be working for him, but he said the magic words that allowed me to remember the Truth about who I was and what I wanted out of life. He informed me that I was his personal family lawyer and that it was up to me to take care of him, his assets and his family. And, at that very moment, I remembered as a child I had always dreamed of being a Personal Family Lawyer. In fact, that is why I went to law school! Now I just had to figure out how to make my dream a reality.

I began to make my experience at The Firm my own. I attended networking events and conferences where I could get to know people, develop relationships and begin to reach out with the hopes that someone would ask me to be their Personal Family Lawyer. I figured if I could build my own client base at The Firm, then I would be the Mistress of my own destiny. It didn't matter to me that The Firm wasn't interested in my small clients (we represented firms like Berkshire Hathaway and Universal Studios!), but it felt right to me and though I didn't know it at the time, I was engaging in **Step Two of Identifying and Realizing Your Dreams: Trust Your Intuition**. My intuition (you know that still, small voice that guides you, sometimes in direct opposition to the loud, real voices that are speaking "at you" from other people) told me to go out and keep meeting people, and things would become clear.

The next sign came as I attended a Women's Business Conference and heard a speaker talking about her business. She was clearly living the life of her dreams. Suddenly I knew there was something more, and I definitely wanted it. At that point, I still wasn't sure what that something more was, but I knew I was closer to finding whatever it was. The speaker had mentioned a coach who had helped launch her business, and while the concept of coaching was foreign to me (and to be honest I thought it was for people who were weak or needed a crutch), I decided to look into it. And, so we get to **Step Three: Be Coached**.

I worked with my first coach for about six months, and I discovered I'd been ignoring what had been staring me in the face all along. Being a business owner would satisfy all of my needs for creativity (I was finally ready to acknowledge that I was creative after years of rebelling against my mom, the art teacher!), allow me to be my unique self, give less to the government, achieve my dream of being a Personal Family Lawyer, and allow me to parent my kids in a more hands-on way than I could driving 40 miles in Los Angeles traffic everyday. Working with a coach helped me to drop the concepts I had acquired as my father's child that being a business owner was only for people who couldn't get real jobs. Ha! What a fallacy that was. Had I remained in my own mind and not worked with a coach, I might still be at The Firm thinking there was something wrong with me!

I began to see there was more possibility, but I still was not entirely clear on what that was, so I asked for help from those around me—even people I didn't know! I decided the best way for me to determine what I wanted was to talk to people who were doing what I thought I wanted to do. So, I called other attorneys who had successful law practices and asked them if they would meet with me. More often than not, they were delighted to help and flattered to have been asked for guidance.

And that is **Step Four: Ask For Help**. As I was interviewing attorneys about their practices, I came into contact with two women, not much older than myself, who were doing it—they had their own law firms, and they were making it happen. These two women inspired me! I knew if they could do it, I could too. So in August of 2003 I launched my own law firm, now known as Martin Neely & Associates, Attorneys and Counselors at Law.

Finally, the last and most important step I took is one that can be hard to follow and it is probably the most important because it has had an impact through each of the other steps. **Step Five: Live Inside the Zone of Discomfort**. I know something really big is going to happen when I am most uncomfortable and most in fear. I've learned to embrace this fear, face it, walk through it, and come out on the other side with more joy than I knew was possible. I was in the zone of discomfort every time I called someone new and asked whether they would meet with me and tell me about their practice; I was in the zone of discomfort the day I gave up my steady paycheck; I was in the zone of discomfort when I opened the doors of my firm with no guarantee of clients; I was in the zone of discomfort writing this chapter and sharing my story with you.

Today, I am on track to grow FAR beyond this little law firm that I created, which two years after its inception has six full time employees and three lawyers besides myself, and I continue to **Follow the Signs, Trust My Intuition, Be Coached, Ask for Help and Live Inside the Zone of Discomfort** everyday.

ALEXIS MARTIN, ESQ. is the CEO of Martin Neely & Associates, a law firm specializing in the protection of your family and your assets. Whether your estate includes belongings of sentimental value only or multi-millions of dollars, you need a plan. Alexis was recognized by Worth Magazine as one of their top 100 lawyers and by Los Angeles Magazine SuperLawyers as a Rising Star. Not sure what you need to do to protect your family? Visit www. martinneely.com NOW for lots of FREE information and guidance.

CHAPTER 8

Do You Mouse Around with Your Power?

MARY ANN MASUR, CPCC

ONE DECEMBER MORNING I was talking on the phone with my sister in St. Louis about what we were going to wear to our respective holiday parties that night. The conversation was abruptly interrupted when I saw a gray little creature scurry across my kitchen floor. I squealed, shrieked and reacted by jumping up and down. From my new found perch on the kitchen counter I could see it move around to the dining room.

After my sister and I stopped laughing, she calmly talked me through the next steps.

Hang up and call Critter Control," she directed. Armed with my broom in one hand and the phone in the other, I called my neighbor instead. As it turns out, she had had a mouse last week and was on her way to Target to buy supplies. This purchase was now doubled. We had our plan of attack.

After my initial hysteria, I went upstairs (safer ground I thought) and called my dad in New Orleans. (Why couldn't this have happened when he was here last week?) Again, after more advice and a reminder that the mouse was scared and would not hurt me, I stepped back to look at the options.

I was giving up my power to this four-inch rodent. I was letting him take control of my house as I tiptoed from room to room. When we react, we frequently give up our power. I am a powerful woman. I speak publicly (the #1 fear people have), I run my own business, and I am a risk taker.

Yet I lost sight of all of this.

When I stepped back, took a few deep breaths and reviewed the game plan, I became proactive. I regained my power. Look at the situations where you give up power. How can you get it back? What happens when you shift from reacting to being proactive? In this chapter we will explore what power means, how we, as humans, diminish or give it up and how we can reclaim it.

Power is often synonymous with control. We think of a hierarchy where those at the top are in control and have the power. They can tell others what to do and others tend to respond out of fear. This is how the feudalism system worked and is true in the military. However, it isn't how power is best expressed in organizations today. Consider the power Mother Teresa had.

Power is about influence. It is getting things done through others, especially when we cannot do it all ourselves. It is treating others with respect and dignity. It is valuing their opinions and letting them speak up. Power is not climbing the ladder on the backs of others, but rather handing them the rope so they can climb on their own in the direction that you chart. It is being able to motivate and lead others toward a desired outcome. It happens when we treat others well and do the right thing.

As a coach, I frequently see accomplished, confident individuals diminish their power, often without even realizing it. We react as I did with the mouse. How do you diminish your power? Let's look at several ways that this happens.

1. **Disregarding our own boundaries:**

   Often we disregard our own boundaries. We let people infringe on our time, interrupt our sentences and step over our needs. We are not even aware that this is happening, but we feel conflict, stress or anxiety. When we do not honor our own boundaries, how can we expect others to respect them? One way to get clear on your needs is to notice those instances when the frustration appears. It is likely that a need is not getting met when this happens. That's when it is time to speak up for yourself and let others know what is important to you. Let them know that you do not appreciate that they are late or interrupt you.

   I had a client who was planning a family reunion and was upset by how the planning meetings were going. It was important for her that everyone treated each other with respect and love, even if they disagreed. She let them know this at one of the meetings and they were very appreciative. One relative even said that she was glad that my client spoke up. By honoring our needs and values and asking for what we want, we set boundaries. We teach others how to treat us and thereby reclaim our power.

2. **Attributing our accomplishments to luck or someone else**

   We often receive a compliment for our hard work and then say, "It was nothing. I didn't really work that hard. The team did." or "I was just lucky." It is important to acknowledge the team, and it is also okay to accept the compliment. When we don't receive credit for what we do or let others know our role in a situation, we give up our power. I coach many executive women who are frustrated when promotions come and they go to men or others. They feel like they are not acknowledged for what they do. Often women are shy about letting others know or taking ownership of their achievements. When we attribute our success to luck rather than our efforts, we play small and minimize ourselves. Luck happens on the golf course. In business, we create our own opportunities and successes which flow from planting seeds and nurturing them with hard work.

3. **Saying "yes" when we want to say "no"**

How often do you say yes and then dread the event or task that you just agreed to? When this happens, we usually feel drained or guilty. Women like to please others and so by saying "yes", we think we are pleasing others. However, we end up being upset and resentful. We have let ourselves down. When we say yes to one thing, we say no to other options. Conversely, when we decline a request, we create an opportunity and space to accept something else. Getting clear on what you are accepting and declining can allow you to stand powerfully in your choice, without guilt.

4. **Reacting to others' agendas**

When we respond to others' agendas without thought, we give up our power. We try to please others and, in the process, lose ourselves. Knowing our priorities and what is important to us can help us stay proactive. We have clarity and focus. When we take a step back and ask for what we want, we honor our needs and boundaries. I had a client who told her Spanish speaking mother that when her mother was visiting in her home, she wanted to keep the TV on English-speaking shows, rather than banish her husband to another room during the mother's visits. Instead of tolerating her mom's visits, she began to enjoy them when she spoke up for what she wanted and the entire family could be together.

5. Sugar-coating

Are you saccharin sweet? I coach many women who sugar-coat their conversations and do not ask for what they want. They think they are being nice. Instead they get frustrated that they aren't getting the results they want. Being direct and asking for what you want is essential to being powerful. It often takes courage and honesty. In the long run, it serves those around you best because you are happier and feel more freedom.

How do you show power? We manifest power in many different ways. By showing respect, considering others' opinions and creating space in interactions, we display power. Power comes from listening to others and their various perspectives. We do not always have to be the one with the answers or telling others what to do. We communicate power in our tone of voice, body language, words and pacing of a conversation. A client of mine once reworded an email response seven times to make sure it had the right tone. She also told the recipient that she was willing to admit that she might not have all of the answers and was open to other perspectives. By stepping back and not reacting immediately to the initial email when it was sent, my client was able to let go of her anger and stand in place of power that put people at ease. She was willing to be wrong, to be open to various viewpoints and to assist in any way possible. By reflecting, taking time to proactively communicate the proper tone and pace and inviting others to participate, she created a powerful result in this outcome.

Power is most effective when we create an environment where others can buy in. It can be tricky because we do not want to be patronizing or didactic. We are able to effectively influence an outcome based on how we treat others. We also stand in our power when we step back and are proactive in honoring our needs and boundaries, when we are direct and ask for what we want. We can be powerful in any circumstance if we choose to, even when we encounter that unanticipated mouse in our house.

⌒

MARY ANN is a certified business coach who works with people who are overwhelmed at the helm to be effective and fulfilled. She has twenty years of business experience focusing on team dynamics and organizational efficiencies. She has served the Baltimore community as an active volunteer and held leadership positions with various organizations. In 2000, The Daily Record honored her as one of Maryland's Top 100 Women. Contact Mary Ann at maryann@synergy-consultants.net or (410) 377-7323. Her website is www.synergy-consultants.net.

CHAPTER 9

The Transition Cycle:
A Comforting Guide Through Unfamiliar Territory

MARCIA MERRILL

WHAT IS TRANSITION?

A TRANSITION IS A TIME in your life when a major change has taken place and your life is adjusting as a result. Changes may be related to the relationships in your life, to your surroundings, to your work life, or to your health and well-being (including your physical, mental, and emotional health).

Some common life changes that may lead you into a time of transition are:

1. Separation from a life partner through divorce or death.
2. Relocation to a new home or city (moving in with adult children or downsizing from the family home to a smaller dwelling).
3. Leaving a job to retire, pursue another career, or to start your own business.
4. Being fired or downsized.

5. Loss of friends or family members through relocation or death.
6. Children moving out and leaving an "empty nest."
7. Retirement of your spouse who is now underfoot more.
8. Health issues such as increased or changing medication needs, increased or changing exercise routines.
9. Lifestyle changes such as trying to quit smoking or drinking.
10. Changes at your job such as a new supervisor or team members.
11. Increased responsibility at work such as a promotion or changing job expectations.
12. Decreased responsibility at work due to semi-retirement.
13. Increased or changing personal development needs such as spiritual or personal growth work, reading, or attending workshops.
14. Revisiting past hobbies or discovering and making time for new hobbies and interests.

Changes happen in our life both as the result of choice and as the result of circumstance. Sometimes you're in charge of making the change (e.g. leaving your job to start your own business), and sometimes the change happens to you (e.g. being downsized or fired from your job).

Transitions are usually easier when we feel we're in control of them—that we've chosen them. But any type of change will evoke some or all of the feelings of anxiety, excitement, fear, foreboding, and uncertainty.

When we're in transition, it helps to know that the period of uncertainty will pass, and we WILL feel our feet on solid ground again. What was new will become familiar. In order to get to that stage of familiarity, each time we go through a transition we need to experience it fully, which means passing through the three distinct phases of the transition cycle.

There's no set timetable for how long this will take, and there's no "skipping" through a phase; each must be experienced fully in order for you to pass through to the next.

PHASE ONE—CATALYST

In phase one, you're actually experiencing the change. Something has happened to you, or you have made a decision and put it into action.

In the catalyst phase, you may feel lost and worried about something that happened, or if it's a change that you've instigated, you may feel confused about whether you made the right decision. You may question everything from your identity to your purpose in life.

Self-expression is a very helpful tool in this phase. Getting your feelings out in an honest way can help you to move through them and on to the next phase. If this transition wasn't one that you chose, try writing a letter to the person or institution that you think is responsible for the change. Vent your feelings until they've all been expressed and released. Then tear up the letter.

Another helpful and enlightening exercise is to write a letter AS that other person or institution in response. You'll learn a lot about another perspective of the situation.

Try injecting some humor into your day when you're in the midst of a recent life change. Lighten up with a favorite comedy tape, cartoon, joke book, or the company of a really upbeat person, and watch your perspective change.

Questioning and uncertainty are a natural part of the catalyst phase of the transition cycle, and lead you into the next phase–cocooning.

PHASE TWO—COCOONING

"Watch me. I'm making a cocoon. It looks like I'm hiding, I know, but a cocoon is no escape. It's an in between house where the change takes place. It's a big step since you can never return to caterpillar life. During the change, it will seem to you, or to anyone who might peek, that nothing is happening—but the butterfly is already becoming. It just takes time."—From *Hope for the Flowers* by Trina Paulus.

Phase two is a "time out"—a seemingly unproductive phase that nevertheless has a very important role in the cycle.

This is time for you to process what's happened and reflect on your life; for you to let go of and grieve for the past, get grounded and centered in the present, and plan for the future.

This is, by its nature, a confusing and uncomfortable time. Though you can't predict or plan when you'll be "done" with the work of this phase, it is possible and effective to take a formal retreat during this time. A weekend getaway, a trip, or just scheduled down time will provide a framework for your self-reflection.

It's helpful to find a way to capture your thoughts as they come–if you enjoy writing, use a journal or the computer for free writing. Or try a structured format like a poem, play, or story. If you enjoy art, try collage, sculpture or painting. If you're musical, write a song or compose a melody that helps to express your thoughts and feelings.

Whichever routine you choose, spend a little time each day coming up with a gratitude page. Write down three things you're grateful for today. It's amazing how focusing on what we have to be thankful for can brighten our mood and change our perspective!

Self-care is also really important in this phase. Be very kind to yourself, letting go of any tendency to self-criticize or place unrealistic demands on yourself. Nourish your mind, body, and soul with pleasurable activities that feel good and are enjoyable to you.

PHASE THREE—COMMENCEMENT

The last phase, commencement, is really a new beginning. It's time for you to embrace new things, embark on new ventures, and live life anew.

You feel your energy building in this phase, and it's still essential to keep up with your self-care and continue to be kind to yourself.

You'll know when you've hit this phase because ideas and possibilities will start flowing through your mind. Your biggest challenge is choosing ONE action to start with.

Instead of trying to do everything and follow-through with all of your ideas, keep a pad of paper and/or a tape recorder close by at all times. Capture your ideas and file them, but be clear on setting ONE action, along with specific baby-steps that will make it happen.

While building and using a strong support network is essential at any phase of the transition, the tool of support can take on a particularly important role in the commencement phase.

The right support structure can provide you with positive role models and gentle accountability to stay on track. Most importantly, make sure you have someone to celebrate with.

Transitions are rarely wrapped neatly up in individual packages. Often life is a series of transitions, and just as we've entered the commencement phase of one transition, we're facing a life change in another area of our life.

The best news is that once you're familiar with the transition cycle, you'll be able to recognize just where you are and just what you need to do in order to navigate through the transition.

MARCIA MERRILL is a Life Transitions/Career Coach with 18+ years' experience. She holds two Masters Degrees (Counseling Psychology & Education) and completed coaching training at the Adult Development Network. She is also credentialed as a Certified Career Management Coach by the Career Coach Academy. To learn about your own "Transition Position"with Marcia the Transition Chick! Book your FREE 25-minute consultation with Marcia to discuss the changes happening in your own life.Email marcia@ecareercorner.com, visit www.eCareerCorner.com or call (410) 467-0811

CHAPTER 10

How To Manage Your Love/Hate Relationship with Time

AMBER ROSENBERG

NOT ENOUGH TIME?

Want more time to workout, enjoy a night out or sit quietly with your thoughts?

If you're like many of my clients who strive to advance in their relationships, careers, and personal lives, you may have mixed emotions about your overbooked schedule; perhaps even a love/hate relationship with time.

You lead a busy life, and you feel if you just had MORE TIME you could overcome the exhaustion and sense of being overwhelmed to create a more balanced and productive life.

If only it were that easy.

Your relationship with time is no different than any other relationship. It requires nurturing and care, and it wants to be valued. Time shows up where it's appreciated and invited. So, perhaps it's time to start managing your relationship with time.

Unfortunately, the phrase 'time management' has taken on a negative connotation. It's often equated with figuring out how to squeeze in as much as possible. This kind of 'time management' rarely leads to a sense of accomplishment or peace of mind—more often, it results in stress, exhaustion and a fragmented schedule that produces few results.

The problem begins when we put too much emphasis on managing time, instead of managing ourselves.

Managing yourself is easy—it's just a matter of focus.

Here's how to get started.

STEP ONE

Try this for the next five days:

Before you get out of bed in the morning, think about your intentions for the day. Instead of immediately tackling your to-do list, first ask yourself:

- What do you want the day to look like?
- What are your emotions around the day (excited, anxious, optimistic, sad, etc.)?
- What possibilities and challenges do you envision?

At the end of each day, think about how the day actually turned out.

- What did you choose to focus on and how did you choose these tasks?
- How do you feel about your choices?
- What is the relationship between your choices and your goals for the day?

At the end of this five day period, reflect back on your observations.

- What patterns do you notice?
- What do these patterns tell you about your goals, priorities and choices?
- What did you learn?

After this five day exercise, you may find procrastination eats up much of your time. Maybe you put off your most important tasks until later in the day, while burning up your morning energy with less important but easier and more enjoyable tasks.

You may discover prioritization is a problem. Instead of looking before you leap, you jump right in to tackle your to-do list without taking the time to prioritize your tasks so you build momentum throughout the day.

Or perhaps you find that you take on too much. You say yes to everything, and as a result, you end up doing many things poorly instead of one thing well.

Setting goals and recognizing unproductive habits are critical steps in learning how to control your day. It's amazing how you can shift the whole feel of the day with just a few minutes of reflection at the beginning and end.

After you have graduated from the first step of setting your goals for the day, try step two.

STEP TWO

Try this for the next five days:

Pay attention to when it feels like you are losing control of your day. Instead of trying to figure out *why* you are losing control, simply be aware, pay attention and be in the moment.

Every time you notice your day is controlling you, stop whatever you are doing, make a check mark and note the time on a designated piece of paper (use the same piece of paper the whole five days).

Then take a minute to close your eyes and ask yourself the following questions:
- Where am I right now?
- What is it like here?
- What is the emotion?

- Where do I feel that emotion in my body?
- What is the weight here?

Simply noticing when you start to go off track is another big step in learning how to control your day. It's a process, so be patient with yourself.

After you have graduated from this second step, you can move onto the third step, which is playing with options and making a choice.

STEP THREE

Try this for days 10-15:

By now you'll be adept at setting goals and noticing when your day starts to get away from you. When you notice it, stop what you are doing, close your eyes and take a minute to ask yourself the following questions:

- What is the cost here?
- What is the benefit here?
- What is possible from here?
- What is not possible from here?
- What other options do I have?
- What option do I choose to pursue?

When you're truly managing yourself, you'll make progress in all areas of your life and be able to maintain balance between work, personal, and family life. You'll have enough flexibility to recognize and respond to good opportunities, avoid pitfalls, and create a sense of ease as you go about your day.

Learning how to manage yourself has many benefits. Here's a good example.

A woman started working with a coach because she wanted to grow her new business while also making time for herself, her family and her friends. She was incredibly passionate about her work and poured all of her energy into it, leaving her with little time for a personal life. She had early morning meetings, and calls with clients throughout the day and late into the night. In addition, she still had to find time to get her 'regular' work done. She had little time to sleep, let alone time for her family, friends or herself. As a result, her relationships were suffering. Not only was she overwhelmed and exhausted mentally and physically, but due to lack of exercise and always eating on the run, her physical health was also in jeopardy.

She realized her current work habits and lifestyle were not sustainable, but she didn't know if it was possible to change anything given the reality of her business. She asked her coach what she needed to do to find peace of mind and balance in her work/personal life, and this became the focus of her work. As a result, she began to realize her priorities, which were quite different than what she had originally thought. It turns out she desperately missed her boyfriend, family and friends and was craving to be outside, exploring nature and moving her body. She decided to better manage her relationship with work so she could re-focus her energy on these other important areas of her life. While her priorities have changed, her business continues to prosper.

Since she first started coaching, she has gotten married and made a commitment not to work on weekends so she can enjoy the free time she "earns" during the week. By better managing herself, she has carved out time for exercise and healthy home-cooked meals. She also cherishes the fulfillment that comes with knowing how to set goals, consider her options and make the best decision.

It was the best choice I ever made.

AMBER ROSENBERG, Pacific Life Coach empowers women in relationship/life/career transitions to create the lives they want to live. Clients include entrepreneurs, professionals, single women, moms-to-be and empty-nesters. She is also a popular speaker, a writer for Know Yourself Magazine and will soon appear in Real Simple Magazine. Amber has 10 years communications experience for Fortune 500 companies and non-profit organizations. Contact: (415) 637-3855 for more information. Sign-up for a half-hour COMPLIMEN-TARY phone session/subscribe to The Confident Woman FREE e-newsletter at www.pacificlifecoach.com.

CHAPTER 11

A Widow's Journey:
From Profound Loss to
Enrichment Beyond Measure
LYNN ROSENBERG

I MARRIED LATE by anyone's standards. In Jerry I had finally found my soul mate. And that was worth those long, often lonely years.

Our nine-year marriage was filled with all the usual stuff...work, travel, friends, disagreements, holiday dinners, misinterpretations, and love through it all.

And then one day, everything changed. The diagnosis: Stage 4 melanoma (skin cancer). It only goes to Stage 5.

Immediately I began to research for treatments. There were none that had been successful. And yet, I hoped.

I was vigilant about his immune system (never planned a social event if a friend had a cold), vigilant about finding—then changing—doctors if I felt the care wasn't caring enough.

Since there was no chemo that was effective, we didn't do chemo...for the first three years. And then it went to his brain.

So I started on the research trail again. Somehow I found a doctor back east who had imported a drug from France that had shown in trials to be of some promise with melanomas that had gone to the brain. I called the doctor, persuaded him to work with us and send it to our doctor in L.A.

Every time Jerry had an MRI, I went with him to the doctor for the results. Oftentimes tests were scheduled on a Thursday or Friday before a holiday, and we'd have to wait four or five days for the results, which was agonizing. I didn't want to think about it yet it was all I could think about. Jerry was much better on this front than I. He wouldn't let himself get scared or obsess about it. He was a brave soldier.

I wanted to help him, but there was nothing else I could do but wait for the next test, the next treatment or the next piece of horrid news.

I did everything I could to prepare myself for *that* day. But as I would come to find out, there is no way to truly prepare. Skin cancer killed him. Silence was killing me. It awaited me in every room.

At night, I would dream he was still alive. When I awoke I was in shock he was gone.

I struggled—with loss, and then four major surgeries of my own.

And when it was over, I realized I needed to either find a job or figure out something I could do myself. I had always been creative and a self-starter. I wrote songs, played piano and sang: I made my living at this for over eight years. Later, I wrote screenplays. I had several screenplays and ideas optioned and had a short film made, which was thrilling.

Now I wanted a business where I could make a living and do some good for others. I had no idea what that might be.

And then I came across a fabric that had UV in it. But what to do with it?

Ultimately, I decided to make small, lightweight, fold-up UV Sun Umbrellas that would protect people from the sun and would also be fashionable. Combining utility with fashion was new—something that was exciting to me.

Every single thing was a new learning experience for me. I knew nothing about making umbrellas, importing or a hundred other things that had to do with business, but through scouring newspapers, trade journals and the internet, I found people with more experience than myself. Most were not only generous with their time, but knowing funds were short, did not charge me.

There were so many stages of development:

- Finding an umbrella manufacturer in China *(who spoke and understood English well enough to communicate ideas back and forth)*
- Getting samples made
- Choosing custom colors for the fabric
- Naming my business/logo *(it took six months!)*
- Finding a graphic designer for little money to create and interpret from me the style and class I wanted for my hang tags and brochures
- Deciding whether my logo, *Soleil Chic*, should be screened on or embroidered
- Creating my website (www.soleilchic.com)
  I thought all you had to do was hire a web guy. (It took me months to write the text and *two* web guys to get it right)
- *Needing to call China almost daily and dealing with big bills later. (You can't hear tone of voice on a fax)*
- Finding a Freight Forwarder so shipping from China to L.A. would go smoothly.

And while the umbrellas were being made, fear raised its ugly head. Terror, really. I began to realize that using an umbrella for sun protection would be an unfamiliar concept in the United States, and perhaps I should have another product to market with it.

So I decided on another, entirely new enterprise for me ... making handbags and totes that would color-coordinate with the umbrellas.

This in itself was an overwhelming learning experience. I didn't know any more about bags than I did about umbrellas.

I used Saks Fifth Avenue and Neiman Marcus as my classrooms, studying their bags for hours and days on end. I would discreetly measure the bags, taking notes, absorbing every detail I could. I would go to textile shows to pick out fabrics. Then I would go to my contractor and she would ask me a million questions, none of which I could answer. So I went back to the stores and studied other details beside bag measurements and types of leather. I had to look at trim, and handle connectors, d-rings, and bottom feet. *(It was like learning a whole new language!)*

Holding my breath, I started to make decisions that would, months later, turn into bags. But I had no idea what they would really look like.

By this point my umbrella manufacturer was taking longer than expected, and I realized I would not have my umbrellas by spring. Or summer. I had gotten my very first order…50 umbrellas from the Ritz-Carlton Hotel/Spa in Pasadena, California. They *had* to be here by summer. If I lost this sale, I'd lose my reputation, even though I didn't have one yet.

There was only one choice. I could no longer plan on shipping them in (literally, by ship). I had to pay an enormous fee to have them *flown in.*

Finally, they arrived. And the moment I laid eyes on them was spectacular. The embroidery was beautiful, as were the umbrellas. *(Later, I would learn that some did not work properly and could not be sold.)*

Meanwhile, my bag contractor guided me, prodded me, and helped me along until my beautiful bags were designed and manufactured. And the first time I saw them, I was excited beyond belief.

I had done it!

Interesting Point: Even though my goal was that a woman would buy both the bag and umbrella, in reality, that rarely happens! But

I'm thrilled with every sale and have received many thank you notes from appreciative women, particularly regarding the umbrellas. They told me they wanted to protect themselves and were thrilled to find my product.

To be perfectly honest, there were mistakes, accidents, and all kinds of challenges along the way. With enormous effort *(and a whole other learning curve)*, I managed to get my products in magazines. However I soon learned that no matter what you're promised, promises can be broken, even at the last minute. Another product can be substituted for yours. Sometimes the company that is most excited about your product decides not to buy. These can be heart-wrenching disappointments.

It has been an exciting, stimulating, frightening experience, and it's not over. New challenges abound each day. But every time I get a new order, or a customer tells me how glad she is that I've done this, I am renewed and know I am on the right path—the path of the deepest meaning and purpose.

If you have lost a loved one, are feeling vulnerable, or just want to start your own business but have no idea what to do and have doubts about your abilities, there are some discoveries I have made that may help you.

1. **STORM YOUR OWN BRAIN** (even more than brainstorming someone else's)

The idea may not come right away, or it may come in a succession of ideas. When I was initially thinking of what to do, I recalled seeing a very well dressed woman walking in Manhattan, carrying a stunning umbrella. I could tell this even though the umbrella was closed. And I thought at that time how great it would be to design something that many women could afford to buy. Maybe they couldn't afford to buy a designer suit, but they could afford to buy one terrific-looking umbrella.

More than 14 years later, that idea morphed into what I'm doing now.

Think of all past and present desires—and combine them with your emotions, loves and losses. Next mix all this with wanting to help others and see what emerges. You will surely come up with something worthwhile.

2. RESEARCH

Stay open to everything: internet, newspapers, asking everyone you connect with in business for a name of someone else who might be able to help with what you need. With research in a variety of ways, new ideas will cross your path. Some may be useless. Others may strike a chord.

3. DON'T GIVE UP!

When I was just about ready to contact China regarding luxury umbrellas, 9/11 happened. Instantly, I thought the idea had to be scratched. Instead I imported American Flag umbrellas. I faxed 35 companies in China and found one incredibly cute design. Stores like Long's Drugstores, Gelson's Market and others bought.

About the time I was running out of umbrellas, I came across the UV fabric. It was only at that point everything fell into place, and my business was truly born.

LYNN ROSE is the founder of SOLEIL CHIC UV umbrellas. After a long career as a pianist-vocalist-composer and award-winning screenwriter, she changed careers after losing her husband to malignant melanoma. SOLEIL CHIC umbrellas have been seen in Skin, Inc., and Les Nouvelles Esthetiques (both spa magazines), Global Traveler, Travel and Leisure Family and in the hands of celebrities like Cate Blanchett. Her umbrellas are endorsed by top doctors including a dermatologist, rheumatologist, plastic surgeon and professor of anatomy and neurobiology. The Mayo Clinic recommends her umbrellas, as well. Top resort/spas such as the Ritz-Carlton, Lake Las Vegas, and The Fairmont Kea Lani, Maui, carry her products. Her worldwide customer base continues to increase every day .Visit www.soleilchic.com.

CHAPTER 12

Frustrated, Stressed and Frazzled? How to Stop it Now!

JEANIE RULE

WOMEN KNOW way too much about stress. Our lives are over-whelmed by it. We spend too many of our precious days frustrated, fed-up and annoyed. As a divorce recovery coach, I work with women who know firsthand about overwhelm, stress and frustra-tion. But in spite of their challenges, these amazing women are determined to live a life they absolutely love—and they use *inspi-ration* to make it happen! I want you to use inspiration too, especially when you're feeling frazzled, stressed-out, and ready to throw in the towel.

Whatever frustration or stress you're feeling right now, the solution is your inspiration. It's always there—it's just up to you to tap into it. When you're inspired, you're moved to do more, think bigger and engage more fully in life. Your life becomes what it is meant to be: juicy, succulent and delicious. Inspiration is like a superhero power—with it, you can do anything!

You may not know this, but you are already inspired. You're hard-wired to be inspired; it's a natural state that's simply been forgotten. Inspiration is much more than motivation. It is a deeply-felt, uniquely personal sensation that you can actually feel in your body. It's an undeniable hunger that you must pursue. Following through on what inspires you gives your life exquisite meaning, purpose and pleasure.

This may sound very 'out-there' but hang on. If being inspired gives you the energy and insight you need to conquer your stress, why wouldn't you use it? Why not pull out all the stops when the chips are down? Begin today by surrounding yourself with what you find inspirational. It can be anything: art, music, places, colors, situations, people, even causes. Whatever stirs your soul is inspiration.

Think back to a time when you were younger, before all the ups and downs of life got in your way. Do you remember being completely wrapped up in your activities? Maybe it was art, or selling lemonade or climbing trees—it was so powerful it was all you could think about, and while you were doing it, you were completely lost in it. That's what being inspired feels like. It's an all-encompassing, creative force that gives you momentum and galvanizes you to take action.

Imagine using that same creative force today—the same one you had when you were a child. Imagine waking up every day feeling completely inspired. What would this do for you? What would it do for those you love? If you felt this way, would you let stress keep you down? No way! You'd have so much more energy and confidence that you'd blast through every challenge and take huge life-changing steps.

To rediscover what inspires you, you must let go of all fear and doubt and become open to discovering what really makes your heart soar. Inspiration never knocks on the door or shows up on demand. You have to give yourself permission, time and space to find what inspires you. You have to make it a priority. You'll definitely know you're on to inspiration when you feel it in your body: you feel lighter, more hopeful and infinitely happier. Here are some suggestions for discovering and nurturing your inspiration.

GROW YOUR INSPIRATION!

Get out and PLAY! We did it as children, and we don't do it enough as adults. Play is the doorway to creativity and creative solutions! Getting out, exploring and having fun is a great way to 'spark' your inspiration. Take a walk, explore a new neighborhood or try something new. Take notice of anything that piques your interest: colors, sights, sounds, people, societal causes, places, etc. Some will hold a passing interest; others will trigger inspiration.

Contribute! We all have gifts, talents and passions that the world needs. If you want to grow your inspiration, spend less time thinking about your desires, and more time serving others. Inspiration is exponential: the more you give, the more it grows. Volunteering in any capacity is a great way to grow your inspiration.

Integrate Inspiration. Give yourself permission to indulge in what inspires you and make it a top priority. Too often we think of inspiration as something we can do after all our other responsibilities are done. It's the other way around! Put your inspiration first, and the rest will follow. The most inspired people I know actually live their inspirations, not just think about them or talk about them.

Adopt a mindset of inspiration. Think inspired thoughts and speak inspired words—this will naturally lead to living an inspired life. Instead of focusing solely on the challenges you're facing, take an inspired approach. Ask, "What can I do to make this situation great for everyone?"; "What are my unique gifts that will enable me to get through this challenge?"; "How will this add something of value to my life?"

Say YES way more often. Every time you say yes (to any invitation that supports your best interests), you open yourself up to experience more of life. Life and inspiration are synonymous. As you experience more life so too will you feel more inspired.

Create environments that cultivate and nurture inspiration. Take a look around. Is your desk uplifting and inspiring, or is it a mess and depressing? What about your home? Do you feel fabulous every time you walk through the door? Who are you spending your time with? Are they inspirational and do they support you in living an inspired life? Do you read inspiring books? Listen to music that moves you? Inspiration thrives when you create the environment to support it.

Take a look at the guiding principles in your life. We all have them—they're our personal views of the world. You may be looking at your current challenges with anger, frustration and fear. Which principles would inspire you to tackle your challenge? Hope, forgiveness and trust are principles that will nurture inspiration and ease your stress.

Make a decision to have inspired principles. A client of mine looked at her divorce with blame, contempt and frustration. After some time, she began to shift. She started replacing blame with acceptance, contempt with forgiveness and frustration with hope. As she spent more time with her inspired principles she felt better, more opportunities came her way, and she was able to fully heal from her divorce.

Just as there are ways to grow your inspiration, there are also ways you can sabotage your inspiration. Here are a few you'll want to avoid at all costs!

SURE-FIRE WAYS TO STOP INSPIRATION

Spend time with people who don't believe in you, value you or support you in living an inspired life. Who you spend your time with is the single most determining factor to your success and happiness. Want to be happy? Spend time with happy people. Want to feel inspired? Spend time with other inspired people. Do your best to end or limit relationships that aren't supportive.

Stick to your routines. Daily routines zap your inspiration! You may be getting the chores done, but it doesn't feel uplifting. You're just going through the motions, hoping that some time in the future you'll live life the way you want to live it. That time is now. In fact, the more you tap into your inspiration, the easier it will be to get your must-do stuff complete. Why? Inspiration is an energizing force that naturally moves you forward. Besides, nothing horrible is going to happen if you shake-up your routines—and you never know who or what you will find as you take a different path.

Worrying about what other people are thinking about you. We all want everyone to think well of us, but this doesn't always happen. You block your inspiration and personal power when you worry about what other people are thinking and saying about you. Do yourself a favor and focus only on what inspires you so you can keep moving forward to create a phenomenal life.

Struggles in life can produce a lot of doubt and fear, two toxic reactions that will immediately kill off your inspiration. The antidote? Develop deep trust in yourself and the infinite possibilities of the Universe. Inspiration is very much an act of faith. You must trust that you know what is right for you, and have the faith to express it. Be courageous and step up to the plate (and remember, your inspired sisters are there with you in spirit!)

It's your birthright to live an incredible, amazing life, exactly as you want it to be! Inspiration will move you past adversity with grace, confidence and pure, absolute bliss. It's your secret weapon to getting what you want out of life! It gives you infinitely more happiness, meaning and purpose—and a powerful tool in abolishing your challenges and stress so you can really soak in the pleasure and joy that life has to offer!

JEANIE RULE is the founder of Solo Mama, a coaching company that helps divorced moms worldwide end the pain, overwhelm and frustration of divorced moms and develop meaningful, dynamic new lives. Jeanie received her coach training at Coach U, the world's foremost coach training academy, and she is a member of the International Coaching Federation and the International Association of Coaches. You can reach Jeanie at (626) 447-7412. Subscribe to her FREE monthly ezine at www.SoloMama.com

CHAPTER 13

How to Build the Life You Want, One Decision at a Time

ELISABETH SAMSON-LEE

WE'VE ALL BEEN THERE. We feel like there must be more to life, that we are not living up to our full potential. We feel as if there is something missing, something wrong with us. We ask ourselves if the lives we are living are the ones that were truly meant for us. We want so badly to make changes. We are not sure what to do, so we do nothing. Or worse yet, we try the same things over and over expecting different results, and when we don't see the results we are promised we label ourselves "failures." We feel like we have tried everything, but have we *really*?

As a society we are encouraged to look for the easy answer, the magic pill, the quick fix. We want it and we want it now, with the least amount of effort and time spent possible. We seem to continue to search for the pot o'gold at the end of the rainbow, even though we know it doesn't really exist. What if I told you that the power to improve your life lies within you, and you can call on it at a moment's notice—whenever, wherever and as often as you like, and nobody even has to know when you're doing it? It is something we all can do. In fact, we already do it all day long. We just aren't doing it as well as we can or with the mindset of bringing us closer to where we want to go.

The key to building the life you want is the power to make good decisions.

I believe our lives are a direct result of the decisions we make. When we make better decisions, we live better lives. As the Decision Diva, I will share with you methods to make it all manageable by turning wishes into decisions, goals into action. We need to take it step by step, decision by decision. No quick fixes. No magic potions. We will just use the power of good, healthy, and focused decisions.

In this day and age, people are totally overwhelmed with information (both true and false). What we really hunger for is wisdom. We are told "knowledge is power." Yes, this is true—though true power lies in the decision to take action. You can fill your brain with all the knowledge it will hold, but what is that knowledge really worth without action? "Choice" is decision without action. "Preference" is choice with no emotion to propel it. "I may" has a much different meaning than "I will." In thinking about the way you make decisions, where do you find yourself on the spectrum?

I have been where you are. I know what it's like. When enough was enough, I began an intense and fearless mission of self-discovery. The journey began over three years ago and continues to this day (and will no doubt continue throughout my lifetime). It has definitely been a crash course in the principles I plan to share with you through these writings, along with various other Decision Diva products I have created and services that are offered. I proudly stand before you a much stronger, wiser, and healthier woman than I was when I began. I am living proof that the Decision Diva system works! Now let me share some wisdom with you.

Let's talk about how to become a Decision D.I.V.A.

Determine what you want.

Do you honestly know what it is you want? If you could do, be, or have anything at all—with absolutely nothing holding you back —what would you want for yourself? Many times we don't even entertain this idea because we let fear creep in the moment we ask the question. We freeze in our tracks due to fear of failure, fear of success, fear of rejection, loss or loneliness, fear of how we look to others, fear of—you fill in the blank.

Or, we do what we do because it is what other people want or think is "best" for us. We don't want to hurt their feelings, right? It would be selfish if we did what we wanted to do, wouldn't it? Sometimes we don't feel as if we have a voice, and when we do, we use it to be "agreeable" and to keep the peace. Who do we think we are wanting these things for ourselves? (Tune into whose voice you hear when these words pop into your head.)

Determining what you want is the cornerstone of the Decision Diva process. If you don't know what you want, how can you make good, healthy, and mindful decisions to get where you want to go and be who you want to be? As you've probably heard before, this can be likened to taking a road trip without a map —not even knowing where you are driving to. Knowing your destination is the most important part (along with gassing up and checking your oil a few times along the way).

Invest yourself in the process.

You must be committed to each and every decision you make from this point forward. All of your decisions are not going to be perfect, though it is vital that you are conscious of each one. Shoot for a ratio of 80/20 in the beginning—80 percent good decisions, 20 percent leeway for not-so-good ones. Remember, the good news is that once a bad decision is made, it's over. There is no need to dwell on it or beat yourself up because the opportunity to make a new decision is right around the corner. You can fix your last "bad" decision by making a great one next time.

Please don't expect to change everything at once! We need to break it down into a manageable process. You can make *one* decision at a time, can't you? That is the glory of this system. Rather than being forced to eat an elephant in one bite, you can see that actual change comes from stringing a bunch of good decisions together. Each decision is a "bite" of that elephant.

Value yourself enough to move forward.

You must truly believe you are worth the effort. Not only you, but others in your life are also worth you living the life of your dreams. Those who love you want to see you succeed. If you are not yet at the place of doing it for yourself, then do it for them.

Take some time to think back over your life and focus on the defining moments—those things that were said or done that made you feel hurt or inferior. You know, those comments where you could literally feel your self-esteem take a nosedive when they were made. Have the courage to look back on those moments and question them. It was impossible to do this as a child, but now it is your responsibility as an adult to look back on those things through adult eyes and ask yourself if they were/are actually true. It may be time to let some of your childhood beliefs go. They have definitely worn out their welcome. This process is actually the most valuable thing you can do for yourself.

It is really important that you take the entire process seriously. Diva status is a big responsibility. And the payoffs are unbelievable.

Action!

You will constantly be presented with decisions to make. Why not be mindful and conscious of each and every one that you make? Why not make it a good one?

When faced with a decision, ask yourself the following questions (and I mean with every decision!):

- Will this decision move me closer to where I want to be?
- Am I making this decision based on what is best for *me*?
- How will my life be better if I make this decision (even better for the next five minutes)?
- Where is this decision coming from (my head, my heart, what I "should" do, or what I really want)?
- How will I feel if I don't make a good decision?
- What will my life look like if I continue to make "bad" decisions?

When an unsuitable decision is made, ask yourself why. (For the record, "I don't know" is not an acceptable answer—dig deeper!)

The glory of this system is that it works in all areas of life—with each and every goal and recycled New Year's resolution—weight loss, increased fitness/activity, stress management, financial health, relationships, career, parenting, life balance, self-care, you name it!

Now is the time to take command of your life. You can do this! You now have the most important tool. We have to decide our way from Point A to Point B, from Point B to Point C. The power of decision is timeless, endless and best of all, painless. Always remember that our lives are a direct reflection of the decisions we make.

ELISABETH SAMSON-LEE is a certified wellness coach and has worked in the health, wellness, and fitness industry for over 10 years. Through her own intense, fearless mission of self-discovery, she uncovered the principles shared in all Decision Diva programs, products, and services. She is living proof that this system works! Please visit www.thedecisiondiva.com to sign up for the Decision Diva Digest, a free biweekly ezine and receive a free special report or call (651) 247-5101 for more information.

⌒

CHAPTER 14

How to Live a Life Filled with Pleasure

DONNA SCHILDER

PLEASURE IS an important component of happiness. It re-energizes, refreshes, and renews us after the hard work of life. It gives us relief from thoughts about our stressors, and it is a reward that gives us the motivation to keep moving toward becoming our best.

WHAT IS PLEASURE?

Pleasure is fleeting, raw emotion that is brought on by social, environmental, and physical factors. Happy social events such as parties, family dinners, and weddings give us pleasure. Environments like Yosemite, a bustling San Francisco street, or Disneyland incite pleasure. Physical factors that create pleasure include eating ice cream, wrapping ourselves in a warm soft blanket, or receiving a hug from someone we love.

We experience pleasure through our senses: sight, sound, touch, taste, smell. Pleasure is a Van Gogh painting, Diana Krall's velvet voice, a kitten's soft fur, ripe strawberries, or the aroma of sweet lavender drifting on a spring breeze.

The pitfall of pleasure is that it habituates easily. This means if you imbibe the same pleasure too much or too often, it has a weaker impact on you. I like to use the example of chocolate. When you take the first bite of chocolate, you feel it melt in your mouth and you taste the bitter and the sweet. You may say, "Hmmm." In subsequent bites, the taste has less impact.

Another example is music. If you listened to Bruce Springsteen's "Born to Run" 24 hours a day, it would lose its positive impact and probably become irritating.

So how do you increase your pleasure?

In the book *Authentic Happiness* Martin Seligman, Ph.D. gives some important strategies for increasing our pleasure:

- Avoid habituating pleasure
    - Spread out your instances of pleasure
    - Enjoy a variety of pleasures
- Savor pleasure
    - Be attentive to the present
    - Conscious focus
    - Sharpen your perceptions
    - Absorption
    - Sharing
    - Memory-building
    - Anticipate pleasure
- Be mindful
    - Slow down
    - Carefully observe the pleasure
    - Sense your surroundings
    - Meditate

SPREAD OUT THE INSTANCES OF PLEASURE

It's easy to get into habits that reduce our pleasure. We go to the same restaurant and eat the same thing, take the same route for our walk every day, listen to the same music, read the same author, play the same sport.

You can avoid habituating pleasure by spreading out the instances of it in your life. If you think about it, if you listened to "Born to Run" just once every Saturday morning, it would probably give you a strong sense of pleasure every time. And even better, you would look forward to it.

ENJOY A VARIETY OF PLEASURES

You can also avoid habituation by seeking a greater variety in your pleasurable activities. One of the first things I do with my coaching clients is help them build an extensive Personalized Pleasure List. We start by looking through a sample list of activities. What does the sample list look like? Some examples from the list include: visiting an arboretum, watching the pig races at the county fair, going to a museum, watching *Saturday Night Live* reruns, hiking in the mountains, watching football, throwing a Frisbee, and flying a kite.

After the client has selected the activities that interest them from the list, we explore questions about pleasure to help them add to their list:

- How do you define pleasure?
- How do you like to pamper yourself?
- What recharges your batteries?
- What thrills you?
- What is fun for you?

- How can you be playful?
- What can you do to your physical environment to have it nurture you?
- How can you contribute to your reserves?
- List 25 things that make you laugh.

The items generated from these questions are then added to the list.

The second step in creating more variety in their pleasurable activities (and spreading out the instances of pleasure) is to help the client look at how they structure their lives. We use two tools: "Your Ideal 14 Days" and "Your Ideal 14 Weeks" to lay out a variety of pleasurable activities throughout their daily life.

This process often prompts my clients to look at what they can cut out or down, so they have more time for pleasure. It also creates a commitment to spending time throughout their week doing pleasurable activities.

It's important to take the time for pleasure. Why? Because not only do you deserve it, but you need it to show up as your best "you" in the rest of your life.

My clients also use their Personalized Pleasure List to choose impromptu activities when they find themselves with some extra time or need to de-stress or re-energize.

It takes some planning, but soon my clients find themselves trying the new Indian restaurant down the street; cooking a recipe they never tried for Mom's spicy meatloaf; walking in the park instead of at the beach on Tuesdays; listening to Ella Fitzgerald, Dave Matthews, Rachmininoff, and the Beatles; reading the *Da Vinci Code*, "Better Homes & Gardens," and *The Road Less Traveled*; and trying golf for the first time. The process really works! Soon they find they are feeling joy like they did when they were 18 and having more energy to face that new project at work.

SAVOR PLEASURE

You can also enhance your experience of pleasure by savoring it. This means having a conscious focus on experiencing it, becoming absorbed by it, and sharpening your perceptions of it.

Instead of going to the beach and getting your walk over with so you can get back to work, you can savor your experience at the beach. Sit on the sand and spend time: tasting the salt air, feeling the gritty warm sand under your toes, hearing the boom of the crashing waves and the cawing of the seagulls, embracing the vastness of the bright blue sky, and sensing the softness of the lazy clouds floating by. Now that's savoring the beach!

Part of savoring pleasure is to sharpen the experience by involving additional senses. Instead of just sitting in the living room, you can light a fire to involve your sense of sight, sound, and smell; you can place a soft pillow under your neck to enhance the sense of touch or drink a cup of "Constant Comment" tea to involve your sense of smell and taste.

Sharing is another technique for savoring pleasure. Have you ever noticed you feel more pleasure in a meal when you are sharing it with others? When you go to a concert with a friend do you find it more pleasurable? That's because you are sharing it.

Memory building also helps to savor pleasure. Talking about a movie, concert, or sporting event afterward builds memories that enhance your pleasure. Sharing memories of family events, with pictures and stories will also help you savor the good times in your life.

Talking about past pleasurable events can also help you build anticipation of future events, giving you optimism about the pleasurable life you will lead in the future.

BE MINDFUL

Mindfulness is another way to increase your pleasure. Mindfulness is careful observation of the present in a slow state of mind. Have you ever gotten into your car and arrived at your destination without being conscious of the journey? This is the opposite of mindfulness.

Being mindful as you leave the house means stopping to notice your spouse's smile as you say goodbye, seeing the flowers in the yard, or seeing the reds, yellows, pinks, and greens of the sunset.

Mindfulness helps you choose not to get caught up in the details of your fast-paced world, so you can have more time to enjoy the gift of being alive.

Some of us numb ourselves through 24 hours a day by blaring TV or radio. Or we never stop working, moving, or doing. This may pull us away from thoughts of our negative emotions such as anger or frustration and the conflicts in our lives, but it also pulls us away from experiencing pleasure and joy.

You can slow down and smell the roses or practice meditation to increase your mindfulness. Meditation can help you practice living in the moment, slowing down, and being quiet. It can also help you embrace silence and stillness so you can allow the beauty that is all around you into your life.

It's not a coincidence that studies show those who practice meditation are happier on average than those who don't. But any way you achieve it, being mindful will help you truly experience pleasure.

I invite you to design a life filled with pleasure by spreading out and creating variety in your pleasurable activities, savoring these precious moments of pleasure, and being mindful of the beauty and pleasure that are presented to you every day.

DONNA SCHILDER, a Mid-Life Renewal Coach, would love to help you design the life you want to live. Mid-life is an exciting time where you can discover new interests, return to old dreams, and re-shape your work-life for greater meaning and flexibility. Contact her at (562)434-7822 or DSchilder@aol.com to experience a free coaching session. Also, visit her website at www.DonnaSchilder.com to obtain free articles on how to design a happier and healthier life.

CHAPTER 15

A Mom's Balance

THERESA VOLKMANN

WHEN I WAS IN MY TEENS my brothers, sister, and I would play a game that would start out with a gleeful cheer, "What are the rules? There are no rules!" we screamed. Our lives were so full of rules it was fun to think we didn't have any.

Now as a mom, I've tried to figure out the rules, and again, there are no rules. Once I gleefully yelled "There are no rules!" Now I quietly question "There are no rules? What am I supposed to do now?"

I know I'm not the only one who feels this way. What are today's "mom guidelines"? Where are those "unwritten rules" written? How do I know what to do, and what not to do?

I started looking at the women I enjoy being around; these are also the ones I want to be like. They all have several things in common; they are happily married, they love being a mom and are doing a great job. They all have their OWN interests, and some of them even have their OWN businesses. I've always been a woman who follows her heart before her head. These women seem to be doing the same thing and most successfully I might add.

What I realized watching the women I admire is "There are no rules!" You don't have to decide to be a stay at home mom and leave the creative work juices behind. The flip side of this is you don't have to be a working mother who only sees her kids at dinnertime. Many women out there are successfully combining the two.

How do they do this? They are successful because they balance their time. Let's use the Family Triangle, as a guideline for balancing your time.

TIME—THE LEGS OF THE FAMILY TRIANGLE

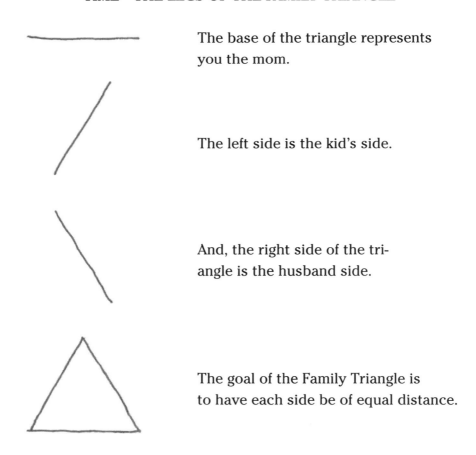

The base of the triangle represents you the mom.

The left side is the kid's side.

And, the right side of the triangle is the husband side.

The goal of the Family Triangle is to have each side be of equal distance.

Are you a mom who does everything for everyone else and nothing for yourself? Then your leg of the triangle we be extremely short. This doesn't give your Family Triangle a good supporting structure, and disturbance from either side could push your triangle over.

Or, are you a mom who is all about your kids? One hundred percent of your effort goes into them. Your leg of the Family triangle is extremely short, the husband leg of the triangle is also extremely short, and the kids leg is long. When you try to make a triangle out of these parts you can't. There is a huge hole that needs to be filled.

Or have you rebelled? Have you decided it's all about you? This would have your leg of the triangle being quite large and the kids and the husband's sides small since the three sides can't connect, the Family Triangle doesn't exist.

Let's talk balance now. When you think about your leg of the triangle, I want you to think about the last time you were on a plane. Flight attendants always tell us in case of an emergency, we need to put on our oxygen mask FIRST, before helping others.

As moms we have to be happy, healthy women so we can guide a happy, healthy family. Being a mom doesn't mean you have to be a martyr. When you start feeling this way, step back and find some refreshing alone time. Find something you love doing, and do it often. This is a time in your life when you can really follow your heart and be passionate about something. Think of the great example you will be setting for your kids if you do this. Your husband will love having a happy excited wife, and happy excited kids. Who could ask for more?

Your kid time is good eyeball to eyeball time. It's reading together, talking and cuddling, cooking together, or a fun outing to the park. When they are home with you they don't need to have 100% of your attention. At different ages the time needed will vary. As a mom, your job is to raise independent, self sufficient kids. On the other hand, it's good to be available when they want to have a discussion on a big issue.

The husband side of the triangle is an often neglected side. The important point to remember is this relationship existed before you had kids; attention and time are required to insure this relationship will exist after the kids are grown. Husband time can't always be eyeball-to-eyeball either. Husband time could be the time you spend budgeting, taking his car to get the oil changed, or running a special errand for him. Make a list of all of the things you can do with or for your husband that falls into this category.

By this point, you have noticed the only things that matter in the family triangle are you, your husband, and your children. Major family decisions should be made with only these three things in mind. My focus has changed from trying to keep everyone happy, to only keeping a few people happy. I'm much more successful with the few.

Now that your lists are made, look at each of these areas as a separate client. The list becomes my project, my objective, and my goal. Now feel a sense of accomplishment, and can pat myself on the back for a job well done. An afternoon in the park with Daniel becomes a mission accomplished, a dinner alone with David is a great goal met, and a solitary pedicure at a spa is an important assignment I need to finish.

Let's look at three real life examples of making decisions with the Family Triangle.

Example One

I decided I wanted Daniel to go to a traditional preschool, not a preschool/daycare. This decision was based on our family values, the entire triangle.

There was a school with a great reputation that Daniel would thrive in. The downfall was it was a 30-minute one-way drive from our house. I would have to take him to school in the morning, drive home to do everything around that house that needed to be done. Then in the afternoon drive to school to pick him up, then drive home again. This decision would make the kid leg of the triangle longer while making my personal leg shorter. Two hours a day driving would take away quality personal time, and it could have possibly taken away from my husband leg of the triangle too. Even though it met our family values, the distance from our house would have put our family triangle out of balance and weakened it.

We found an in-home traditional preschool 1/4 mile from our house. They only accept ten kids and have two teachers. Six boys Daniel's age from our neighborhood would be attending. The kid leg of the triangle is stronger and I get personal time, so my leg is stronger. Choosing this preschool for our son strengthened our family triangle, and everyone was happy.

Example Two

This year Daniel is going to afternoon Kindergarten Monday thru Friday. Monday, Wednesday, and Friday he goes to preschool in the morning. The preschool committed to giving Daniel lunch and taking him to Kindergarten. It was brought to my attention however, that on these days Daniel wasn't always at school on time for kindergarten. Being on time is something that's very important to me and is something I want to instill in Daniel.

I had set up this schedule so I could have three full days to get my personal time in, and also handle more family errands and tasks. When I heard that Daniel was showing up late, I knew a change needed to be made.

What we decided was that I would pick Daniel up at preschool, have him eat lunch in my car, and I would get him to Kindergarten on time. At first, I worried about my leg of the family triangle. This was an odd time to be taken out in the middle of the day. What would happen to the errands and other things I wanted to accomplish? But because of my feelings about being on time, I decided this was a good trade off.

We have been doing this for the last five months. My leg of the Family Triangle is fine; this time really isn't taking away from my personal time. The kid leg of the triangle has been strengthened. Daniel and I are really enjoying the half hour middle of the day check- in time. I'm going to miss it next year when he is in school all day long.

Example Three

Alone couple time is a must! Family or a trusted babysitter needs to be nurtured and used. Grown up dinners and weekends away are necessities. Have you convinced yourself that your little ones can't live without you? The first time David and I went away for a weekend, I remember calling home to check on Daniel. I braced myself for a tearful "Mommy come home." Instead I got "I'm having fun!" It was harder on me to be away than it was for Daniel.

The kid leg of the triangle will be just fine, if you take occasional getaways with your husband. Your husband's leg of the triangle will be greatly strengthened, and your leg will be reinforced.

I'm going to leave you with the challenge to balance your family triangle. I hope you noticed my examples were nothing extreme, it could have easily gone either way without any horrible repercussions. Each little adjustment brings you closer to being a happy, balanced mom with a happy, balanced family.

THERESA VOLKMANN, the Mom Mentor, has been married to her husband David for 10 years and is the mother to six-year-old Daniel. They all live, work and play in Northern Nevada. Theresa readily admits she has made a lot of mistakes, and learned a lot of lessons over the last ten years. She has finally found her stride, her balancing point and she is ready to share what she knows with you in her free weekly ezine. To subscribe go to www.MomMentor.com.

CHAPTER 16

"Count Your Lucky Stars"™

"Enrich Your Life One Blessing at a Time"™

JACQUE WEISS

I'VE ALWAYS BEEN known to be a positive and upbeat person. I was always the "Kool-Aid" mom—the mom who stayed home, took care of the home and family. You know—the cook, groundskeeper, carpenter, school volunteer, etc. I had a part-time job and was the full-time caregiver for both sides of the family. I gathered up the neighborhood children and everyone had fun, including me.

Then, several years ago, I went through one of life's toughest challenges—divorce. This was a life-changing situation that hit me hard and fast. My world was devastated, and my morale was extremely low. Things seemed to be very bleak. I was falling deeper and deeper into that black hole—emotionally, physically, spiritually, and financially. I had no hope or light.

I felt as though I had some kind of disease that was slowly taking my life from me one agonizing day at a time. I knew I had to do something quickly to keep my daughter, Lauren, from falling in the hole right along with me. We've always had a great mother/daughter relationship; together day in and day out, with a bond that seemed unbreakable. Yet from all the stress, cracks were beginning to show in both of us, and immediate repair was necessary. I was using whatever energy I had left in me not to let my despair show, but my "fake it 'til you make it" motto was wearing thin.

When I was home by myself I could release my fears through gallons of tears and let myself breakdown and crumble to nothing. Then I would have to gather up the pieces and try to put myself back together the best I could. The most difficult thing to do was to put on a happy face and pretend that everything was great, and that I had everything in control. I had to do this every day when I walked out the door into the real world, or whenever Lauren was in my presence. I didn't want her to see what was happening to me—I was embarrassed because I've always been the rock.

Needless to say, this was exhausting, and I struggled every day to make it through, worrying about what the next day would bring. I would ask myself, "How much longer can I keep up this charade without going over the edge?" I would tell myself, "I'm the adult; I must be strong." Knowing in my heart that I was becoming weaker and weaker, I couldn't bear to ask for help—that would be the lowest of lows for me.

My faith in a higher power was out of reach. I asked for guidance and vowed to do whatever it took to make our surroundings loving, safe, and better for the both of us. Then I had that one "smack upside the head" day. Something hit me hard—a strike of lightning—a whirlwind—some type of sensation that opens your head and heart to new possibilities!

My inner voice was yelling at me, "HELLO...! Take a look around! If you would release that negativity you would see what wonderful and precious gifts surround you. You would be able to recognize all you have to be thankful for."

Then I thought, "Okay, okay I'll listen." Again I heard that little voice sing, "You should *count your lucky stars* that you and Lauren have a great love and respect for each other. You have a roof over your head, food to eat, heat to keep you warm, running water to drink and to bathe in, and so on."

Wow! Now there are a few happy thoughts! Hmm, that's a different way to look at it. Instantly I was encompassed with a feeling of warmth and love. It knocked me to my senses, and it was the beginning of something big! There was NO TURNING BACK!

I know sometimes when we try something new it seems like it's going to kill us. Well, I knew if I didn't try this new way of thinking, the negativity was going to get me. I decided I would give it a chance and try to *count my lucky stars*. I would find at least five things daily for which to be thankful and see what happened.

Counting my lucky stars started working with me, and I began to feel better about things. Since Lauren and I have always loved making up games, I figured maybe we could make one out of this. We could take turns sharing at least five things each night we were thankful for as I tucked her into bed. We looked forward to our nightly bedtime chats. It was my way of giving her a sense of security and abundance of love, and truly hoping she would have sweet dreams. For myself, I found comfort that "I had made it through another day."

When we first started doing this we found all the good obvious simple things in our day. We were thankful for gas in the car, our home, food on the table, a bed to sleep in, and a pillow to lay our heads on. No matter what, we would stick together and live with what we had and not worry about what we needed or wanted. One of Lauren's lucky stars was that her friend was able to come over and play or spend the night. She was grateful that she was able to continue to attend her private school. She was concerned about leaving her friends behind and having to start over in a new school. A huge lucky star for her was that we didn't have to move out of the house she grew up in. She loved being here and saw it as her safety net.

As the nights progressed, so did the amount of our lucky stars. Our five things grew. We would say to each other, "No, wait I have another one!" Then the other would say, "No, I have one better than that." We had so many lucky stars that it would keep us up way beyond our bedtime. We decided we would share 10 each with one another, and then we would complete our own lists as we laid on our pillows in our own beds. It became a nightly challenge of who could be more thankful. At the conclusion of our list together, I would tuck her in saying, "*Count your lucky stars*, I love you BIG! Sweet dreams, I'll see you in the morning." She'll never be too old for me to share those important thoughts with her, and to this day, Lauren still remembers this!

As time went on I realized we needed to find the positive within the negative situations also. I tried to explain this to Lauren in a way she could understand. I told her I would be thankful if I had a flat tire in town. With a look of confusion on her face she asked, "Why would you be thankful for a flat tire?" I told her I would be thankful because it happened in town where I could get help quickly, not on the highway where I would be going at a faster speed and possibly endangering others as well as myself. Ahhh…she got it! When your child is able to comprehend what you're sharing—that's a huge "*lucky star!*"

We began to add to our collection of lucky stars in a new and exciting way. It's amazing how many things we can find to be thankful for. Maybe we dropped a glass and it didn't break, it's sprinkling outside but we made it in the door just before it poured down rain, or we found ourselves at the store with a cart full of needed groceries and it just so happened that we had one check left. By changing our focus, we were able to reverse the negative things in our day and turn them into positive blessings.

Counting our lucky stars has enriched our lives, one blessing at a time. It will magically transform yours as well.

"COUNT YOUR LUCKY STARS"™

Here's to counting *your* lucky stars on your journey in life wherever it may lead you.

On the days when
your heart and soul seem to be shadowed,
look above the clouds,
for the sun is always shining upon you.

Each choice, each thought can be changed.

Look back and capture
the grateful moments in your life.

Look forward to
beginning and ending each day by
counting your lucky stars.

-JACQUE WEISS

JACQUE WEISS created "Count Your Lucky Stars"™ to help people enrich their lives one blessing at a time. She is an Enrichment Expert, speaker, author and entrepreneur who inspires women like you to find happiness in life, and create a future filled with possibilities! Her top priority is her daughter and considers "being a mom" her most rewarding experience. Visit her at: www.CountYourLuckyStars.com to share your "Lucky Star" story and to sign up for your free email Enrichment Minute. You may also email her at:
Jacque@CountYourLuckyStars.com

PART II

BUSINESS AND FINANCIAL

FULFILLMENT

⌒

CHAPTER 17

How to Go From $50,000 per Year to $50,000 per Month While Working Less and Having More Fun

ALEXANDRIA BROWN

WHEN I LAUNCHED my first business seven years ago as a marketing communications consultant, I had no clue what to charge, how to market myself, or how to run a profitable business. As a result, I attracted overly demanding clients whom I slaved away for; I worked like a dog seven days a week, and I could barely pay the meager rent on my crappy pre-war sublet in New York City.

My cash flow was completely UP and DOWN. One month I'd get a bunch of checks and pay down my bills... the next month I was broke once more, clipping coupons, racking up debt again, and considering moving back in with my parents in the Connecticut suburbs.

I felt like a BIG FAKE.

The last straw was the day I couldn't even take out $20 from an ATM because my balance had gotten too low while I was waiting for a big check from a client. I broke down and cried in the bank lobby, feeling embarrassed and hopeless.

I thought, "If this is what it's like to own your own business, I want to go back and find another job!"

Fast forward to my life today—things are VERY different! I'm writing this on my laptop computer from the sunny balcony of my luxury waterfront home in Marina del Rey, California. I drive a brand new sporty convertible. I enjoy the services of a house-keeper, errand runner, chef service, and a personal trainer. I take quarterly vacations and fly first class everywhere I go. I routinely write checks for thousands of dollars to my favorite charities.

How can I do all this now? Because my business now brings me an average of over $50,000 a MONTH. (Yes, a MONTH. And occasionally even over $100,000 a month!) That's more cash in a typical *month* than I made in entire *years* of my earlier career!

So what changed?

Did I start a whole new business? Did I get involved in a "get rich quick" scheme? Did I take out a giant loan and open an office with 20 employees? Did I work even harder or more hours?

Nope, nope, nope, and nope!

All I DID was change my BUSINESS MODEL.

You see, I SHIFTED from an "hours for dollars" business model to one that leverages my KNOWLEDGE and EXPERTISE—not my time.

This NEW business model does not drain me, but instead EXCITES me, helps THOUSANDS more people, brings in much more INCOME, and gives me tons more FREE TIME. And I'm still using the same knowledge and expertise I was using for my consulting business.

And YOU can do this too!

The SECRET to this shift was discovering how to leverage **email, the Internet, and information products**.

Obviously this shift didn't happen overnight. There is a distinct formula and process that I took YEARS to figure out, because NO ONE else is teaching it! So I now share this program in detail, which I call my "Online Success Blueprint."

The process is quite simple, yet quite detailed. But to get you headed in the right direction, here are a few things you should think about changing NOW:

1. Become Known as the Expert in Your Niche

Experts are more respected, get media attention, get paid more, and get less price resistance (meaning people are happier to pay you what you ask). I went from being a general marketing communications consultant to one who specialized in newsletters. Then in email newsletters.

Then I took it a step further and dubbed myself "The Ezine Queen." I had no idea at the time how much that would help me get famous and be remembered. Did you know that Muhammad Ali became known as "The Greatest" because Ali himself said it? Yep—he just kept saying it, and then eventually so did the media!

There's a reason people happily pay more to get advice from the wise woman at the TOP of the mountain! (Meanwhile the chicks at the bottom can't even seem to give it away.)

2. Build a List of Your Ideal Audience

STOP marketing one-to-one, and START marketing one to hundreds, thousands, or even *hundreds of thousands* of people who are your ideal clients and customers! The hands down best tool I've used to build a list of 20,000+ clients and customers is by publishing an ezine (email newsletter). It's easy and free, and for such a simple tool it's deceptively powerful.

My ezine is the core of my entire business, not only driving most of my income from resulting sales, but also positioning me as an expert, getting me worldwide publicity, and spreading the word about my products and courses around the globe. And it's a SNAP to publish!

And now that I have a built-in audience to market to, I can generate "cash on demand" anytime I have a new product, course, or workshop to sell.

3. Raise Your Rates

This may seem like a given, but you wouldn't believe the resistance I get from clients when I poke and prod them about this. Example: Last year, I hired a personal trainer who only charged $50 an hour. He often complained that his schedule was so jammed it was killing him. To make a living at that rate, he obviously had to take on clients morning, noon, night, and weekends. He was such a good trainer I would have gladly paid him $100 an hour for his time. I remember suggesting he raise his rates, and he replied, "But then not as many people would work with me."

But that's the idea! Let's say he decided to double his rates, and half of his clients dropped off. Why wouldn't you want to work HALF as hard as you are now for the same income? (Hmmm...) This also opens up more time for you to work on new projects, like creating information products and courses that will make you a lot more money for your time.

4. Restructure How You Work with Clients

Instead of taking on one-shot projects, work with clients on retainer (a set fee per month) or require them to sign up for a certain number of months with you. One trend in coaching and consulting right now is moving toward six-month or annual contracts. Not only does it help guarantee your cash flow, but you attract better, more qualified, and more committed clients.

Example: After I tired of doing so many one-shot consultations with people, even at $1,000 an hour, I created my Private Platinum Mastermind coaching program. Out of dozens of applicants I took on only 15 members at $15,000 per year. This program allows me to work with only a handful of serious solo-entrepreneurs, coach them closely over several months, and mastermind together at our live meetings. It's especially rewarding for me to see my clients implement the recommendations I make, follow along with their progress, and share in their successes! (And once I get this group going I will launch another one.)

5. Create and Sell Information Products!

Here's the hard honest truth. You simply will never make the big bucks if you keep getting paid solely for your time. I'm at the point now that about 95% of my income comes from selling my knowledge via information products such as e-books, manuals, courses, audio programs, and occasional live events. This has helped me increase my income over the past three years by 400%!

Instead of "work, get paid"...you want "work, get paid, paid, paid, paid, paid, paid, paid, paid, paid!" I may spend a good chunk of time creating a new product, but then it can sell forever. I may put a lot of effort into creating a one-time seminar, but I also record it and create a home-study version that can sell forever. (I did this with my recent Online Success Blueprint Workshop.)

Start Looking at Your Knowledge, Expertise, and Time Differently.

I hope you get the idea! There are many other strategies to leverage your knowledge into income without working so hard, but these are great ways to get started. Remember, it's about SHIFTING your current business model into one that gives you more money, time, and freedom!

*Online entrepreneur and marketing coach ALEXANDRIA BROWN, "**The E-zine Queen**," publishes the award-winning weekly **Straight Shooter Marketing** ezine with 20,000+ subscribers. She's creator of the "**Online Success Blueprint**" system and the "**Boost Business With Your Own Ezine**" system, designed exclusively for solo-pre-neurs. If you're ready to jump-start your MARKETING, make a lot more MONEY, work LESS, and have more FUN in your small business, get Ali's FREE WEEKLY TIPS by going NOW to www.EzineQueen.com!*

CHAPTER 18

Financial Literacy:
Investing in the 21ˢᵗ Century
CHRISTINE N. CIBULA, MS

FINANCIAL LITERACY is one of the most difficult skills to acquire. We are not taught money management on any substantive level until perhaps college. Finances at that level still seem like an anomaly. Business accounting and finance classes are components of financial literacy but merely as tools of analysis. They do nothing to teach us how to invest, make a return on our investments, or manage risk. Most of us were never exposed to basic principles of investing or financial literacy even at the undergraduate and graduate college level.

WHAT IS FINANCIAL LITERACY?

Financial literacy consists of three components:
1. Debt Management & Elimination as well as Assets & Liabilities
2. Streams of Income—Employee, Self-Employed, Business Owner
3. Investment Portfolio—How to make your money work for you through a variety of investment strategies. These can include,

but are not limited to, investing in other businesses as a venture capitalist, investing in real estate, and investing in the stock market.

These components may seem like overstating the obvious, but in truth, many people never put it all together under the umbrella of financial literacy. The purpose of this chapter focuses on the third financial literacy component—the investment portfolio and investments in the stock market.

INVESTMENT PORTFOLIO & THE STOCK MARKET

I have met many successful businesspeople who understand the importance of leveraging their finances by making their hard-earned capital work for them. However, when push comes to shove, they turn their hard-earned income over to a financial planner whom they rarely talk to. In most cases, they have some kind of preliminary meetings to discuss the importance of "diversifying their portfolio" and then rarely, if ever, do they have contact with their financial advisor. Most businesspeople freely admit this to me whenever the topic arises. It goes something like, "Yeah, I can't remember the last time I talked to my financial advisor. I don't even open my statements anymore!"

What makes matters worse is that even though they have put their money into an account that is supposed to be earning capital for them, they soon discover not much capital has been earned on their behalf. If anything, they may have lost up to half or more of the money they originally placed into mutual funds. This is a dangerous place to be, because we tend to avoid what is painful, most especially loss. Hence, we tend to put off looking at the balance on the statements, often times leaving them unopened.

THE FINANCIAL PLANNER AND
MORE QUESTIONS THAN ANSWERS

Many clients are first-time investors. They take their hard-earned money and place it in the hands of a well-respected financial advisor at a brokerage firm. Typically, there are no other financially literate people in their lives to ask questions. Hence, they do not know what questions to ask their financial advisor. Here are a few starter questions to get you going:

1. Can you explain how to read my monthly statement to understand what is happening with my investment over time?
2. What exactly does it mean to diversify my portfolio? Further, how do I know if I am diversified in the appropriate manner to be maximizing my income potential?
3. What is the difference between an IRA and a ROTH IRA?
4. How does an IRA differ from a RMA (Resource Management Account)?
5. What are the benefits and limitations of each type of account?
6. Is it better to invest in a mutual fund or in specific stocks?
7. How do I know when to cut my losses and get out of a mutual fund or a stock?
8. What stocks are in my mutual fund?
9. What is a realistic ROI (Return On Investment) I can expect?
10. Where do I get started to get these answers?

Most of us are ready to run for the first sale or spa treatment we can find in order to avoid the pain of what I call the "Level One" investor questions. We get overwhelmed and relegate it to something to get to after trash and taxes. This is not because we are uninterested. It is because we are intimidated and confused. The system is designed so you ask as few questions as possible and interfere as little as possible. This should not be the case.

THE TRUTH ABOUT INVESTING

The role of the financial advisor is to place the investment capital into a "diversified portfolio" that minimizes risk while providing a consistent return on the initial investment. A diversified portfolio with mutual funds in various sectors balances out where the money is invested in the market. One goes up and the other goes down, keeping the portfolio "balanced." Unfortunately, you don't make much money with this approach. Meanwhile, your financial advisor collects a commission on your account every year whether you make money or not.

This system is designed to keep a level of distance between an investor and his or her financial advisor, ensuring just enough ambiguity to keep you guessing while not challenging the status quo. Individual investors keep the stock market liquid and provide a stable floor when there are significant changes in the market in order to prevent a stock market crash and another Great Depression. Of course, the inherent benefits of being an investor outweigh the risks. Stock market savvy is important now more than ever as the social security system fails and Baby Boomers steadfastly approach retirement without long-term retirement income. In short, your livelihood and quality of life depend on financial literacy.

TAKING INVESTMENTS INTO OUR OWN HANDS

Most of us stop there and never get to "Level Two" investor questions. These questions are for the more sophisticated investor who has taken a leap away from a financial advisor and put his or her money into a trading account through a brokerage firm like Charles Schwab. This can be a dangerous place to be if you do not have an in-depth understanding of the market. This translates into, "You *can* lose the shirt off your back."

In most instances, the Level Two investor is open to greater risk of substantial loss or at least a faster and more obvious loss than the Level One investor who will likely break even or lose money over time, such as when the bull market bubble burst. Level Two investors need to learn how to be savvy stock traders, starting by learning the basics:

1. What are the differences between the NASD and the NYSE?
2. How is my stock or mutual fund performing relative to the market?
3. How do I buy/sell short and when do I sell/buy back?
4. How do I look at charts and track my money's performance?
5. What tools do I need and how often do I have to do it?
6. What is the difference between technical and fundamental analysis?
7. How much and what specific technical analysis do I need to know?
8. How much and what specific fundamental analysis do I need to know?
9. How do I manage risk?
10. How do I protect my initial capital investment?

HOW TO MARRY THE BEST OF BOTH WORLDS
FOR FINANCIAL LITERACY

"So what do I do and how do I proceed?" is the most frequently asked question I receive. First, be honest with yourself about where your investment skills are and live within those parameters as you are learning. Second, take steps to move you in the right direction.

Become a Financially Literate Investor

1. Learn how to read your statement.
2. Evaluate "What's Important Now" based on where you are in the here and now by taking a realistic assessment of your stocks and mutual funds.
3. Learn vital investment information and skills.

Learn How to Have a Productive Relationship
with your Financial Advisor

1. Become financially literate. Know what questions to ask your financial advisor in order to make solid financial decisions regarding your future.
2. Keep track of your progress over time and hold yourself accountable. Make changes as necessary by staying aware of and connected to your investments.
3. Design an effective partnership with your financial advisor so you can both experience the value of the relationship.

Individual investors earn income on their income, making their money work for them. However, just like with a business, if you had an employee who was not performing for you, you might choose to replace that employee with one who does. Business is business. Consistently losing money is not an option. Consider what it took to make that income.

You do not need to become a master trader to master your finances. What you do need to know is how to figure out where your finances are at any point in time. You need to manage your investments with the kind of confidence and business savvy you use to manage your professional life. Financial literacy is not a luxury. It is a necessity that will provide long-term financial wellness in the years to come.

⌒

STRATEGIC LIVING, INC. (www.Strategic-Living.com) is a San Diego based Business Consulting Firm. Consulting services include financial planning, business infrastructure planning and development, operations and project management, marketing, media relations, and targeted search engine optimized press releases. Clients come from a variety of businesses, but they all have one thing in common. The information, products, and services they offer serve to better the world, one life at a time. ***Register for a FREE 30-minute consultation: www.Strategic-Living.com/freeconsultation.html.***

CHAPTER 19

Discover the Five Keys to Business Success and Fulfillment

KATHERINE CIBULA

AS SHE TURNS 60 this year, the baby-boomer woman is once again in the midst of a revolution. She is one of the most powerful forces in America today. The baby-boomer woman has seemingly accomplished it all. Since the days of bra burning and the Women's Liberation Movement, she has gained power in the workplace, prestige in the community, financial freedom and affluence. She is well educated, well traveled, and well heeled. Seemingly, she has managed to have it all, at least on the surface.

But dig a little deeper, and you will find some unrest. "Is that all there is?" she wonders. Frequently, her life circumstances have changed. She may experience the unexpected loss of her job. She may be in transition in the aftermath of divorce or death of a spouse. Or she may simply not be ready to begin her retirement years, and is searching for a new direction in her professional life.

Whatever circumstances bring her to this point, she finds herself at a crossroad. On the verge of entering this new stage in her life, she is looking for a second chance. A second chance to become the person she was meant to be, bring more meaningful experience to her life, and to leave a lasting legacy behind. Her self-imposed challenge is to live her life with greater purpose.

The Baby Boomer woman is once again leading the charge in this revolution. Her desire to make manifest a more meaningful contribution through her work is changing the way we will view and accomplish our work. This phenomenon, however, is not exclusive to the baby boomer woman. Increasingly, women of all ages are seeking to experience deeper fulfillment in their personal and professional lives.

Are you searching for deeper meaning in your life?
Do you want to make a difference in this world?
Are you seeking greater opportunity for self-expression?

As a business consultant to entrepreneurs, my focus is to help each client clearly and specifically identify core beliefs. My goal is to help uncover unique intention. The following five keys are the foundation for designing a business model that applies the power of intention.

FIVE KEYS TO BUSINESS SUCCESS AND FULFILLMENT

- Intention
- Purpose
- Vision
- Passion
- Mission

Through thoughtful examination of each of these key concepts, the path to business success and fulfillment becomes increasingly more clear and personal. By digging deep into your psyche and spirit, you will identify your source of personal fulfillment. Once you have successfully identified this source, you can begin creating a business design that embodies these qualities. Let's examine these five keys in detail to understand their relationship.

Intention

Intention is the source of all creation. "In the universe there is an immeasurable, indescribable force which shamans call intent, and absolutely everything that exists in the entire cosmos is attached to intent by a connecting link," writes Carlos Castaneda. In his book, *The Power of Intention*, Dr. Wayne Dyer quotes Pantanjali who more than 20 centuries ago suggested, "Dormant forces, faculties, and talents come alive, and you discover yourself to be a greater person by far than you ever dreamed yourself to be." So it is with Intention. By naming what we intend, we give it form and substance in the universe through thought.

"Thoughts are things," counsels Napoleon Hill in his book, *Think and Grow Rich*. Nothing can come into existence without intent. It is the first step to finding success and fulfillment. Think about your intention. Visualize it.

What is it you intend to create?
Who do you wish to benefit?
Why is this of importance to you?

As you uncover your intention, you will begin to see a vision emerge that continues to become clearer the more specific you become at defining what that "IT" is, unique to you. Develop a powerful intention statement. It will keep you focused on the goal you intend and the outcome you desire for your life and your business.

Purpose

Consider asking yourself these questions to discover your Higher Purpose:

- What am I here on this earth to do?
- What do I hope to accomplish?
- What motivates me?
- What unique gifts do I possess that I can share with others?

What do you value spiritually, emotionally, physically, and financially?

Discover your Higher Purpose, and you will be on the Path.

Vision

Close your eyes and meditate on your Vision.

- How does it look?
- How does it feel?
- Who do you see benefiting from your vision?

Imagine the future you intend to create. Envision yourself as having already achieved your dream. How do you feel as you imagine your accomplishment?

Clarify your Vision to gain insight into your dreams.

Passion

- What stirs your soul?
- What excites your enthusiasm?
- What ignites your desire?
- What do you have intense emotion about?

Discover your Passion. Love the life you have imagined.

What can you spend hours doing and be so absorbed that you do not notice time going by?

What are your unique natural talents? What are your gifts?

Think back to what you loved doing as a child. I have had the good fortune to meet many highly successful people. One common characteristic many share is that the work they are most passionate about in their adult life is directly related to a childhood passion.

"My work is my play, and my play is my work," Martha Stewart explains. She attributes her successful career to her love of cooking and the domestic arts, which she happily developed as a child growing up. Consider how seamless the transition between work and play can be if you are doing the work you love.

Mission

- Define your mission.
- Write a mission statement.
- Who will benefit?
- How will it be accomplished?

Your mission will become very clear as you successfully identify your intention, purpose, vision, and passion.

FROM INTENTION TO ACTUALIZATION

Gaylene Anderson is creator of the award-winning water safety learn-to-swim DVDs, "Waterproof Kids" and "Baby Steps." My client's personal account clearly illustrates the power of intention.

"I was a graduate student in Health Education," Gaylene begins. "I had been struggling with developing an idea for my thesis in public health. One day, I was at home studying and watching Oprah. That day, her guest was a young single mother of three who had brought her family off welfare through the creation of a successful instructional video on how to play guitar. The young woman advised, 'For women going into business, find something you really love, that you know well and have experience in. Find a way to help others. Then it will never feel like work.' "

Intention Uncovered

"My passion was in public health, and my love was always swimming," continues Gaylene. "I had years of experience as a competitive swimmer and coach. At that moment, as I listened to the young mother on Oprah, I remember thinking, *I can do that!* I realized I could do what I love most, which is swimming, and teach people life-saving water safety skills in a learn-to-swim video. So I wrote down my intention for a business idea onto paper that very day."

Higher Purpose Discovered

"I was deeply concerned about the alarming statistics of accidental drowning in the Hispanic and African American communities. They are nearly double the national average. My intention was to make water-safety and swimming available to everyone, regardless of economic status or geographic location."

Vision Clarified

"My dream was to find ways to reach populations that were not being served. I wanted to create a product that would meet their needs by providing the instruction for life-saving water-safety skills in an easy to follow format and at a price most anyone could afford. By partnering with major distributors, Waterproof Kids DVD is now available nationwide. We are expanding globally, with Waterproof Kids and Baby Steps being translated into several foreign languages."

Passion Communicated

"Of course, it didn't happen overnight. I had to meet the right people who shared my vision to partner with," explains Gaylene. "You've got to have faith and keep moving in the right direction. I remember thinking to myself, I know there is a greater purpose, a bigger plan for what I want to accomplish. I just have to listen to my heart, and believe."

Mission Defined

"Our mission has grown and expanded to prevent and protect children from accidental drowning. Waterproof Kids is dedicated to providing fundamental life-saving techniques of water-safety and swimming education to children of all ages and economic circumstance."

"Thanks to that young mother on Oprah, I set out on the path to discover the work I love and found it!" smiles Gaylene.

Create a business model that reflects who you are at your core. As an entrepreneur, the opportunity to build a business that is in alignment with your core beliefs and values is limitless. By gaining a deeper understanding of your innermost dreams and aspirations, you can build a business that will manifest your desires. It will drive your business to greater success. These opportunities await you as an entrepreneur.

KATHERINE CIBULA is Vice President of Strategic Living, Inc., (www.Strategic-Living.com) a San Diego based Business Consulting Firm. Focused on the empowerment of the small business owner, comprehensive services include targeted search engine optimized press releases, marketing, media relations, business infrastructure planning and development, company operations, project management and business consulting. **Register for a Complimentary 30-Minute Consultation: www.Strategic-Living.com/freeconsultation.html**

CHAPTER 20

Add Cha-Ching
to Your Business

CHERYL E. COOK

HAVE YOU EVER tossed and turned at night, wondering how to get more cash in your business? Has advice to improve your cashflow, like speeding up collections and slowing down payments, left you looking for other ways to add oomph to your bank account? If you're a small business owner like me, you need creative yet practical ideas on how to bring more revenue into your business that have little or no cost and are easy to implement.

EXPAND YOUR MARKET WITH PAYMENT OPTIONS

You may have unknowingly limited your market size by choosing to accept payment by cash or check only. Ophthalmologists found this to be the case when lasik eye surgery initially became available. A procedure not covered by most insurance plans, the initial market for the procedure included only those who had substantial savings or several thousand dollars in cash to pay for the procedure. Admittedly, this limited the market size.

In order to expand their market, ophthalmologists offered a

payment option which included an up-front partial payment, with the remainder paid automatically in installments from the patient's bank account. By offering this payment option, more patients were able to afford the procedure by spreading the cost over time. Is this an option for your clients?

GENERATE REPEAT BUSINESS

Generating repeat business should be a big part of your marketing plan, unless of course, you're a grave digger. For everyone else, selling products and services to current and past customers costs less than attracting new customers.

By offering a discount on services, you can generate repeat business. Let's say you offer five oil changes for the price of four. (I love discounts!) The easiest way to manage this is with a stored value or loyalty card. If you're familiar with gift cards, they work the same way. The loyalty card is loaded with $125 (five oil changes) for a cost to your customer of $100 (a $25 discount) paid at the time they get the card. Then, as the customer returns to redeem their oil changes using the loyalty card, you have a chance to offer them solutions to their additional needs such as an air filter, a PCV valve or a coolant system flush. Every time the customer visits is a chance to increase your revenue from repeat business.

Amusement parks use a similar method for securing repeat business by selling season passes. Every visit to the amusement park is an opportunity to generate additional revenue. While revenue from the season pass is one revenue stream, return visits generate additional revenue from:

- Parking
- Refreshments
- Memorabilia

Offering customers prompt pay discounts is a reward for faster payments, but it can also be used to encourage repeat sales. By allowing the discount to be calculated on the next purchase rather than deducting it from the current payment, your customer is encouraged to pay invoices early, and to make another purchase in order to redeem the discount. For example, an early pay discount of 5% would be earned by the customer when the current bill is paid within 10 days. The discount—say, 5% of $1,000, or $50— would be used as a deduction from their next purchase.

Both credit and cash customers could earn a discount on their next purchase. I experienced this recently on a website where each purchase generated what they called a "pay-it-forward" amount to be applied to the next purchase. While I didn't earn a huge discount, it's just enough to make me return for future purchases.

SPAWN NEW REVENUE STREAMS

Gift cards have become the gift of choice for those hard-to-buy-for friends and as a perfect thank-you gift to business associates where another gift would be too personal. No longer only for the retail giants, gift cards offer advantages for the small business owner.

- Recipients of gift cards tend to buy at full price rather than sale items.
- The business gets use of the funds on the gift card until it's redeemed.
- Shrinkage encountered with paper gift certificates is eliminated since gift cards have no value until initialized at the time of purchase.
- Unused balances are an immediate addition to the bottom line.
- Gift card recipients often purchase more than the card value, adding to the revenue already generated.

Another twist on the gift card is using it for customer refunds. I bought gifts of jewelry for friends in my wedding and then found something I liked better. By the time I got around to returning the original purchase, the store's credit policy allowed an exchange rather than a cash refund. So, I got a stored value card (looks and smells just like a gift card). Now, I have just $2.72 left on that card.

Whether I make an additional purchase to use that last little bit on the card or pitch it and forget about it, the business wins. If I don't ever redeem it, that's incremental cash for the business; if I do use it, the purchase will be significantly more than the card balance.

By packaging your existing products with a higher level of service you create another revenue generator. For example, your office machine business might offer a "premier" package which includes 24 hour service and a free loaner should their machine need to be sent in for repairs. Customers pay a monthly fee for this premier service and peace of mind. The cost to provide the service is low for the business owner, yet it has the potential to generate additional monthly income.

ADD VALUE

How good are you at communicating the value your business provides? Does your invoice simply list the products or services and the invoice amount? What about the application fee you waive? ...Or the extra hours you don't bill your client? My invoice used to simply list the products and services I charged the client. When I revamped my billing system, I also added the products and services normally provided to my clients without charge. Now, both the products provided at no cost and those for which there is a charge are listed. All are listed with the market rate and a "no charge" notation next to those for which I don't charge. With this approach, the customer can see two things:

- The value of the products and services provided.
- The fact they were not charged for these products and services.

Unless you list those phone calls, mailings, or extra hours you provide at no cost, your client won't have a true picture of the real value you provide. Since an invoice is one piece of communication your client is sure to read line by line, use it to your advantage to build value and loyalty to your business.

A commercial cleaning business recently reported they'd had a customer call to cancel service. The business had just initiated a program to inspect each customer's location once a month to uncover any quality issues, but somehow had missed this customer.

What should you do if a customer calls to cancel service? Well, have you ever tried to cancel your newspaper subscription, your phone or your cable? These companies offer incentives to keep you as a customer because they realize the value of retaining customers. To keep the customer who wanted to cancel, the cleaning business could have offered:

- A complimentary carpet cleaning of the reception area.
- 20% off their next bill.
- Another valuable product or service to say "I value your business and want to keep you as a customer."

If you have a cancellation on your hands, do whatever you can to retain that customer (and your cashflow).

I have a number of pens with my company name and address imprinted on them. I bet you have some with your business name, too. We probably got them the same place—our mailbox. They are free samples we got from a promotional items company who is betting once we see the product in our own hands we'll want to order pens that we can give out. When I considered hiring a business coach, I got a free coaching session giving me a chance to experience coaching. Just like holding the pen with my company name on it, I could see what it would be like to have a coach.

While I'm a big advocate of taking advantage of these 'free' services, you should be the one offering 'free' products or services. To fill the pipeline with prospects, you'll want to give prospects ways to see what you're all about that have no barrier to entering the pipeline. What can you give away for free or for a low cost that gives your prospect a chance to take your products and services for a test drive? Once your prospects take your business for a test drive, they'll be hooked, just like I was after my first complimentary coaching session, when I became a paying client.

Increasing your cashflow isn't about creating new widgets, but about seeing the possibilities hidden within your own business. Use these ideas to increase revenue by leveraging the assets you already have.

CHERYL E. COOK has a passion for helping others. This was evident when she overcame a fear of the water, moved to the Caribbean to teach scuba diving, and used empathy to increase sales at a Caribbean hideaway. Cheryl now uses that same passion along with her 26 years experience in financial management to help small business owners bring more cash into their business. A complimentary e-book, "50 Ways to Increase Cashflow," is yours at www.promoneyinc.com/ChaChing.htm.

CHAPTER 21

Communicate with POW!er

MICHELLE Y. DRAKE

IN MY COMPANY they call me "The Velvet Hammer." My communication style is direct and to the point—but compassionate and caring as well. In order for a woman to advance in the business world, communicating with confidence and poise is a requirement. With confidence comes power...with poise comes control. All of this tempered with the feminine touch creates a collaborative environment ripe with the ability to effect change.

Communicate: To convey information; to reveal clearly. To have an interchange of ideas. To express oneself; to be readily and clearly understood.

Power: The ability to perform effectively. Strength or force exerted. The ability to exercise control. Having great influence over others.

DON'T BE A 'FRAIDY CAT!

When I was in college, there was a class that I enrolled in called "ROTC-Leadership." At eighteen, I did not know what ROTC stood for, but I soon found out. I was expecting to study important leaders in history and their communication styles. What I got was running, shooting guns, and obstacle courses. The last straw was the final exam: jumping off a five-story science building. My fear of heights had me in a total panic. This exam was the determining factor for an A or an F in the class, and failing was not an option.

I have to confess that I tried every trick in the book to worm my way out of jumping. I tried pleading, crying, playing sick and even threatening to pass out—certainly not communication techniques that I would endorse in the workplace today nor ones that worked on that rooftop in 1979! The captain who taught the class didn't buy any of it; instead, he talked to me until I took the leap.

This nightmare turned out to be a defining moment for me. I felt power surging through my veins as I stood on the ground and looked up at the height from which I'd just jumped. It felt as if light and energy were shooting out of my fingertips, and in that instant I knew I could accomplish anything that I set my mind to.

The fear I'd felt manifested itself into a powerful belief and a bold inner voice echoing through my mind: *I can do this...I can do anything!* I've been afraid since then, but now I believe that I can get past any fear because I have the power to overcome, the power to triumph, the power to jump off a building.

Confronting that fear gave me the tools to handle other more traumatic events that life had in store for me. I use this experience as a measuring stick to gauge the obstacles in my path. Every time one threatens to stop me, I think to myself, hey, I jumped off a building—I can handle anything!

One of the first steps to communicating with power is to overcome the fear that blocks you from saying what's on your mind. How many times have you wanted to express yourself but let fear hold you back? How many times have you wished later on that you had had the courage to speak your mind? Think of everything that you've accomplished in your life. Feel the power of your own inner strength and will. Draw upon it, break down the barrier of fear, and communicate!

WORK BACKWARDS!

When I coach my clients on communication, we start by overcoming their fears and move onto discussing how they can powerfully communicate their ideas. I start by asking these questions:

1. What outcome do you need from this conversation, presentation, or meeting?
2. What action should the listener take?
3. What should they know about you or your message?
4. Who is going to be your listener?
5. What are you most afraid of happening during this conversation, presentation, or meeting?
6. How much information can you retain? Cut that in half and assume that is the capacity of your listener.

Once you've answered these questions and have a clear picture of this interaction and the end results, you can prepare for it in a way that has you poised for success.

PERSONAL *SWOT* ANALYSIS

The most powerful communication is communication that taps into who you are as a person. I have a client who came to me for coaching on a presentation she was scheduled to give to college students. She is a filmmaker and had created a film centered on a political message. She planned to speak to the group about that message but wanted to position herself as a role model and someone that they could relate to—not just another activist on a soapbox.

In order to be able to communicate powerfully and effectively with this group, she had to understand, as a speaker, her strengths and weaknesses, the opportunities this presentation was giving to her, and her threats—the places she might find obstacles to conveying her message.

*Her **SWOT** Analysis looked like this:*

Strengths:
- The ability to tell stories
- Visual presentation skills
- Film as resource
- Youthful appearance

Weaknesses:
- A focus on only one project
- Lack of experience speaking

Opportunities:
- To inspire young women into action
- To gain feedback on film

Threats:
- Audience short attention span

We developed her program based on this analysis. The presentation began with a viewing of her film. It was a testament to what she was able to accomplish with her passion and talent. Then we managed to her strengths: we let the film speak about the political issue, and she told her story of how she went from student activist to filmmaker. She balanced her strengths and weaknesses, her opportunities and threats and presented a powerful and inspiring program that touched the hearts and minds of the young people listening to her.

Knowing your SWOT will help you grow into your best communication style, and when it all comes together, you will feel the surge of your own power.

WATCH YOUR WORDS—SPOKEN AND UNSPOKEN!

Too often, we as women in business hand over our power to male colleagues simply by choosing the wrong words to convey our messages. Word choice can either empower us or put us into a submissive role. Choosing words that show action will project a more confident and controlled presence in any interaction.

Weak Passive Words:	Strong Action Words:
Impact	Shrink/Grow
Share	Discuss
Chat	Examine
Spend	Invest
Very, very important	Critical/Vital
"…as soon as possible…"	"…by September 1st"

And don't forget about your body language! It visually cues the listener on over 80% of information that is communicated. No matter how strong your words might be, weak body language can weaken your message. Be aware of your eye contact, your hand movements, and how your body is positioned while you're communicating. Take action and choose the words and body language that say POWER to express yourself and your message!

TECHNIQUES FOR GETTING WHAT YOU WANT!

The following are simple techniques that you can employ to effectively communicate what you want—and then get it:

1. Think about exactly what you want before you say a single word.
2. Use a story to paint a picture of what you are trying to express.
3. Remember who is listening and what style they respond best to.
4. Know what your listener's hot buttons are and USE THEM.

5. Be observant of speakers whose styles you admire; then test them out yourself.
6. Don't forget to LISTEN!
7. Stay on track with your goal!

REMEMBER THE OLD SAYING: "PRACTICE MAKES PERFECT!"

Some people are lucky enough to be born naturally powerful communicators. Clearly conveying their message comes easily to them. They never seem to search for the right words or freeze up. For the rest of us, however, it takes practice to communicate effectively.

The first time speaking about a concept, you might get tripped up with word retrieval issues (tip-of-the-tongue syndrome) or stutter or go off on a tangent and lose your place.

The second time out loud, you can correct your course and make adjustments. Pinpoint problem words or areas and work through them. Is there an area that's slowing you down? Tighten it up.

By the third run, you're as smooth as silk—your message rolls off your tongue easily.

Practice the rule of three: for every one conversation, presentation, or meeting you have, practice what you want to say at least three times with yourself—and enjoy the feeling of communicating with power when you can get your message out there easily!

You can communicate with power in any situation and with anyone: bosses, colleagues, clients, family and friends. Utilize these tips and techniques and watch your career soar!

MICHELLE Y. DRAKE is an internationally-known professional speaker and business strategist with over twenty years experience and is currently president of The Cove Group, Inc.—a management consulting firm. Drake also hosts a weekly business talk-radio show. Her expertise in human motivation and communication has provided tangible solutions to Fortune 100 companies, start-up entrepreneurs and individuals seeking personal and professional guidance. For information call (860) 536-4959. Visit www.michelleydrake.com for a free mini-course.

CHAPTER 22

Attracting Your Perfect Customers

SYLVA DVORAK, MS, CHES, PhDc

INTRODUCTION

- Would you like to have all perfect business relationships?
- Would you like to be able to earn more from your current customer base and/or business builder network?
- Would you like to stop trying to figure out ways to pursue and obtain new customers?

If you answered yes to the above questions, what I am going to be sharing with you in this chapter is an introduction to a powerful system for attracting the perfect individuals to you.

HOW I CONNECTED WITH
THE UNIVERSAL LAW OF ATTRACTION

In 1998, I started my own business and experienced success quickly. "Success" is relative, and for me at the time, making well into six figures defined success. In those early days, my business was primarily international. I traveled extensively, running as fast as I could to provide quality services for my clients. I was doing business in different countries and flying to the east coast each month. I was conducting a large social marketing campaign in Northern Brazil while pursuing business in Europe and Australia. You get the picture...I was busy taking care of my customers and growing the business. Then it happened! My business "crashed" and there I was, sitting alone in an 1,800 sq ft office wondering why? Of course, as life often happens other parts of my life "crashed." I call it one of my "moments of awakening."

In spite of this painful experience, I kept doing and trying what I had done before; the same things that I believe had resulted in my previous success. This time, once again exhausted and at my lowest point, I stopped running in circles long enough to ask: Why is what I am doing not working like it did before?

Then it dawned on me. I realized that working hard was not what I needed to do to make my business and life successful; I already knew how to do that, and it did not make any difference. The "work harder and longer" model did not bring the results I was looking for. Nor did it bring me the happiness I believed came with success.

In fact, "working hard" is only 10% of business success. The other 90% is what is "in your head"—our beliefs or our belief system. These are often self-limiting beliefs that inhibit or just plain stop us from achieving the success we so strongly desire.

What I had known so well and worked so hard at, was the traditional form of marketing. I didn't know it was only 10% of the game. The other 90% I now realize was in my head, and it was about my own belief system.

Almost as soon as I had this realization I met (or attracted) Jan Brogniez and Stacy Hall, authors of *Attracting Perfect Customers-The Power of Strategic Synchronicity*. They introduced me to the

Universal Law of Attraction, and from them I learned how to apply it in all my relationships, both personal and business. In one of the greatest "aha" moments of my life, I realized this was the missing link, the other 90%! The key I'd been looking for!

THE UNIVERSAL LAW OF ATTRACTION

There are laws that run this universe, and the Universal Law of Attraction is THE foundational law. Without an understanding of this Law, none of the other laws of the universe will work for you. What is the Universal Law of Attraction? It is simply that "like attracts like" or, "birds of a feather-flock together." This natural and universal phenomenon of attraction can be seen at work in all physical and social sciences as well as in the healing arts; it equally applies to the fields of business and marketing.

Particles are attracted to other particles and so create atoms. Stars, galaxies, and solar systems emerge from gaseous clouds that swirl into coherence, creating new forms of energy and matter. Humans reach out to one another and create families, tribes, and work organizations.

Attraction is the organizing force of the universe...Attraction has created the universe as we know it. Our thoughts are actually vibrations. It is through vibrations that the attraction happens. And, clarity transforms us into powerful magnets, each automatically attracting others who have the same intention.

How many of you have had the experience of getting clear on something and then it somehow "magically" starts to appear in your life? You think of someone and they call; you need some information and then you hear someone say something that points you in the direction of what you are looking for...this is what I am talking about. Wouldn't it be great if you could attract your customers or any relationship just as easily? I have, and you can too.

ATTRACTING PERFECT CUSTOMERS

Have you thought "I need more customers." If yes, consider this…

85% of new businesses fail within the first five years of operation, and, of those that survive, another 85% will fail within the next five years. The major contributing factor to these failures is that these businesses have focused their resources on finding or "targeting" customers to serve.

There is a common belief held by most business owners that all of their business problems would be solved if they could just figure out the secret to "finding and keeping more customers."

And, this is their biggest mistake!

The never-ending search for more customers requires an abundance of people, time, and money…resources that are usually in short supply in most businesses. In such an environment, the effort put forth to "find" customers is actually draining the business of its energy, creativity, and enthusiasm…valuable resources required to serve existing customers in a satisfying way. Since dissatisfied customers do not return, the business must keep finding NEW customers to replace those they have lost.

Remember the 15% of businesses that succeed? They structure their business in a way that "attracts" only perfect customers and clients. I invite you now to replace the thought, "I need more customers" with the absolute conviction that "I now attract only perfect customers."

What's the difference?

It's the difference between a successful business and one that struggles to survive. It's the difference between a profitable business and one that pinches pennies. It's the difference between a thriving business and one that is hanging on by a thread.

THE LIGHTHOUSE TEST

How can you tell if your business is structured to "attract" customers?

There is a simple test. It's called the Lighthouse Test.

Imagine a lighthouse standing strong and erect on the rocky shores of a beautiful ocean. On this particular day, the water is calm, the sky is blue, and there are many boats out to sea. Yet, out in the distance, there is a storm cloud forming on the horizon. It is coming closer to shore very quickly. The sky is getting darker, the waves are getting rougher, and many of the boats are being tossed about on the water. As the rains and the winds pick up strength, so does the power of the beam of light emanating from the lighthouse. Some of the boats, anxious to move quickly to a quiet and protective harbor, are relying on this beam of light to guide them safely to the spot. The darker the skies become, the brighter the light shines.

Please also notice that not all of the boats are in need of this beam of light to guide them to safety. Some have more confident captains and crew, while other boats have equipment that can handle the storm effectively.

Now, imagine that the lighthouse gets upset because some of the boats are choosing not to come to its harbor. Because it wants to protect and serve all of the boats in the sea, it sprouts arms and legs and begins running up and down the beach, waving its arms, doing its best to catch the attention of all the boats. What would be the result?

Most likely, the boats that were depending on the light to guide them would by now have been destroyed in the chaos and confusion caused by the light moving up and down the beach. Other boats, led by their curiosity, may come closer to shore to get a better look at the spectacle of a lighthouse running up and down the shore, and then head back out to deeper waters. While others would be perfectly content to stay where they are...out at sea. The end result, very few boats are served safely and securely.

The test lies in asking yourself, as a business owner or manager, how often are you the lighthouse standing securely on the shore attracting boats (customers) to you with your light, and how often are you running up and down the beach looking for boats (customers)?

When you look for Customers to Serve, you find "Customers from Hell."

When you look for people to serve, you expend a lot of energy. First, you have to figure out where you are most likely to find the greatest number of customers. Then you must spend more time and money experimenting with the right way to catch their attention. Once you've caught their attention, you then must convince them that you have what they want. By the time you have actually found someone who is willing to try what you have to offer, you are exhausted!

So, when this customer tells you they are not completely satisfied with your products, your policies, or your pricing, you are more than willing to make compromises to satisfy them...truth be known, you are simply too tired to put up a fight. Thinking you have won the war, you feel you can afford to let them win these smaller conflicts...especially in light of what it would cost you to go out and hunt down another customer to replace this one.

The truth is that if we had more strength and solvency, we might all be more willing to listen to the tiny inner voice that says,

"Be careful...this one could be more trouble than they're worth. This is a customer from hell."

Yet, we all have ignored this inner voice because we needed to make back the money we spent on our marketing and sales program. Or we convince ourselves that these customers must be perfect for us because they responded to our advertising or clicked on our hyperlink, or we were afraid that the competition would serve them if we didn't. Inevitably, though, the inner voice was right; by the time we ended our tortured relationship with this customer, we felt that no amount of money in the world would have been enough to compensate us for the cost of the experience. We blamed the customer for the poor quality of the interaction.

The truth is, as business owners and managers, we are solely responsible for who we choose to serve. When we create advertising campaigns or promotional strategies that fail to clearly convey the bright light of our unique business distinctions, we find customers that other businesses should be attracting and serving. As soon as we hear that inner voice warning us that we have found a "less-than-perfect" customer (for us), it's a signal that our own distinctive light has gone out. It no longer has the power and brilliance to attract only perfect customers and clients.

Take a moment now to picture one of your most perfect clients—the one person with whom you most enjoy working. If you're like the majority of business people, the client you describe as perfect is the one who respects and values your time. They trust you to have their best interests at heart and come to you with realistic expectations; they happily pay what your product or service is worth. They are intelligent, trustworthy, and sincere, and refer you to friends and family; they help build your business. Perfect customers make you feel needed, appreciated, respected, and understood. More importantly, they reconnect you with the passion and purpose that put joy in your work—the very reason you got into your business in the first place. When you think about it, these perfect clients often come to you easily; there was an immediate spark of attraction and connection with this client as if synchronicity brought you together at the perfect time and place.

So...are all of your clients or customers perfect? If your answer is "no," then consider a new marketing model...one that transforms your approach, attitudes, and behavior to create the synchronicity that easily attracts perfect clients and customers to your business.

> *"Man is made by his beliefs. As he believes, so he is."*
> —THE BHAGAVAD-GITA

*Currently, SYLVA DVORAK is consultant with Amazon Herb Co. As a refugee from the former Czechoslovakia, one of Sylva's life passions is to help others find their own personal freedom within whatever context they live or work. To help you create a Strategic Attraction Plan for relationships in your life and business contact: Sylva Dvorak at (310) 454-7478 or (310) 614-1828; sylva@atmanint.com; www.amazonabundance.com Thank you Jan Brogniez, Alan Hickman, Chris Attwood and Janet Attwood for your continued love and support. The best-selling book, **Attracting Perfect Customers...The Power of Strategic Synchronicity,** is available at www.perfectcustomers.com.*

⌒

CHAPTER 23

Minding Your Own Business

AMI DWYER, ESQ.

WHATEVER YOU ARE doing, you'd probably like to be more relaxed and confident that what you are doing in your business *right now* is just what you need to be doing, and know that the business itself is in top form. Like the perennial statement, "I should really have a will," (and you should!) on every business owner's "To Do" list is a group of items that never seem to get resolved. It becomes an elusive list of things that need to be "figured out," and unfortunately year after year, the "To Do's" remain permanent fixtures on the list.

Failure to take action on these "To Do" items is not only a continual drain on your energy, it exposes you and your business to countless unnecessary risks. To run an efficient, profitable, and secure business that allows you to sleep well at night requires you to *mind your own business*. Here are 8 STEPS to take NOW to help you get started.

1. FORMALIZE YOUR BUSINESS ENTITY.

Many businesses start small and without the formality of becoming a legal business entity. This is unlikely to be advantageous legally or tax-wise. A business that is not formalized is a sole proprietorship. This means that the individual who owns the business (and all of that individual's property) is exposed to the risks the business incurs.

Other forms of businesses are partnerships, S or C corporations, and limited liability companies. Each of these entities has the advantage of legally distinguishing you as an individual from your business. As one of these entities, if your business was to incur financial losses or get sued, you the individual would likely be shielded from personal responsibility and your personal assets protected from attachment. Your lawyer or accountant can advise you as to what structure is most advantageous. Even if you are solo, a formal business entity is important protection for your personal assets.

To form a business entity, either contact your lawyer (it is less expensive than you would think), or a savvy individual could do it using the application forms available on the local state department of assessments and taxation website. Once formed, make sure to learn what is required to comply with the law for that entity (annual meetings, minutes of those meetings, among other things), and keep current on these requirements. If you are unsure of what is mandatory, your lawyer can teach you how to comply with the requirements.

2. TREAT YOUR BUSINESS LIKE A BUSINESS.

Open a business account at your local bank solely for your business. Keeping the money flowing through your business separate from your personal finances will avoid additional tax return preparation and bookkeeping costs. It will also allow you to protect the benefits of your business as a separate legal entity. This division will insure that, should a problem arise, you as an individual and your personal property will not be impacted by actions your business takes.

3. GET AN EMPLOYER IDENTIFICATION NUMBER.

Just like your social security number is your personal identifier, your employee identification number (EIN, or Federal Tax Identification Number) is the number used to identify a business entity. You will certainly need an EIN if you have employees, are a corporation or partnership, or if you fit into certain other categories. Using your EIN is yet another way of identifying your business as a separate entity from yourself. More information about employee identification numbers is available at www.IRS.gov.

4. BUILD YOUR TEAM.

Chances are you are an expert in your field, but you are not a bookkeeper, accountant, or banking professional. Find a trusted professional in each of the fields needed to round out your own experience and expertise through research or referrals. Interview people before hiring them to be certain they are familiar with the kind of business you own, so that they understand your needs, and are prepared to guide you and teach you what you need to know to run your business effectively, in addition to performing their designated tasks.

5. BUILD A RELATIONSHIP WITH YOUR LAWYER.

A lawyer who is familiar with your line of work and whom you trust is a valuable ally. Are you incorporated? Do you have or need an operating agreement? Does your field have licensing requirements? Do your contracts protect you? Are you complying with wage and labor laws?

Operating a business raises many kinds of legal questions and learning opportunities. Just like a "well-visit" to the doctor, having a lawyer you trust to check in with periodically or to call upon for advice is invaluable, whether or not you have a legal "problem." And when a problem does arise, you will have someone to handle it promptly and efficiently.

As with other "team members," your lawyer is in the business of providing *personal services*. Your lawyer should be a trusted advisor. If you are not getting personal service from your lawyer, or if you are uncomfortable asking questions or getting the information you need, find a new one.

6. GET INSURANCE.

Buying insurance is a relatively inexpensive way to protect the business you have worked so hard to create. Many kinds are available—for professionals in certain fields (lawyers, accountants, doctors, engineers)—there is Errors and Omissions Coverage (E&O) for professional negligence (malpractice). For most other businesses, there is Commercial General Liability Coverage (CGL), which covers general negligence of a business. In addition, coverage is available to protect your property, inventory, and many other aspects of your business. For most businesses, a CGL policy with a million dollars in coverage is available for a fraction of what one would expect.

What do you get for this investment? In many cases, if your business gets sued for something covered by the policy, the insurance company will hire a lawyer to represent you and will pay any settlement or judgment that is obtained against your company. Spend some time with an insurance broker familiar with your line of work to evaluate what kind of insurance is available and how much coverage is needed to provide adequate protection for your business and its assets.

7. DELEGATE.

For every task that needs to be done ask, "Am I the best person to be doing this?" Knowing your strengths and weaknesses and what is the highest, best use of your time, is an important skill for a busy entrepreneur. If you are not good with numbers, hire a bookkeeper. If you have data that needs to be entered, hire someone to do it. If you aren't good with technology, find someone who is.

Often, the only way to grow a business is to let others handle those tasks that you don't absolutely need to handle personally.

8. . . . BUT DON'T LEAVE IT ALL TO THE EXPERTS.

While numbers 7 and 8 may sound contradictory, they are not. In order to effectively understand how your business operates, its profitability and level of efficiency, you must delegate to team members you can trust, but above all, you must also mind your own business. Ask questions. Familiarize yourself with each part of your business so you know what is required, how long it should take, and what it should look like. If there is something you don't understand, pay someone to teach you.

Ultimately, your business is your dream and your responsibility. Don't risk losing your legal protection by failing to maintain your business. Failure to pay taxes or required fees to your state department of assessments and taxation can risk your company's legal status.

Minding your own business inevitably leads to a more efficient, profitable, and secure business. Knowing you understand how your business is operated, it is compliant with the law, its assets are protected (as are your personal assets), and you have a team in place to teach, guide, and provide you with necessary services will lead to increased peace of mind and the knowledge that your business is built on a solid foundation.

Just as you have a choice about how to live your life, you have a choice about how to run your business. You can either continue to leak precious energy by failing to "mind your own business," or raise your standards and take action. Minding your own business, treating it with the level of respect and professionalism it deserves, may be the very thing needed to communicate to the world that your business is ready to take it to the next level.

⌒

AMI C. DWYER, ESQ. is a partner in the law firm of Franklin & Prokopik, P.C. in Baltimore, Maryland, an educator, communicator, and coach. Her vision is for every business, large and small, to have a trusted legal advisor. As a steward for her clients, Ms. Dwyer helps businesses manifest their vision through sound business planning and risk management. In addition to her work as a lawyer, Ms. Dwyer is also a mother of four, a pioneer in the area of work/life balance and passionate about community building. She can be reached at ami@amidwyer.com.

CHAPTER 24

Leading From the Inside Out

SARAH A. FERMAN, MBA, LMFT

POPULAR OPINION has it that leaders are born and not made. I sat in LAX waiting to Board a four and one half hour flight to New Orleans where I was going to meet my daughter. In less than 48 hours my 27 year old was going to have a life saving surgery that was paradoxically life threatening.

Had I guided her into the right decisions? The right mindset? Had I taught her the art of asking the right questions? Had I taught her the art of listening? Was I a leader? Do I have what it takes to lead her through this? Did I have the fortitude to help her? Did I have the flexibility to help my family through this life challenge? Can I lead them without managing them? I certainly know the difference; because I help people learn how to do this every day. I am a busy competent woman, with places to go and things to do. What would be the best way to handle my clients, students, employees, and myself through this time period?

I struggled with my ability to help my daughter and family, while juggling my life at the same time. My career has been spent working with leaders within the business community and the community at large, and now I am wondering what kind of leader I am. How did I develop these qualities? Does the woman sitting next to me have them? How about the lady taking the boarding passes or the woman getting her four kids ready to pre-board?

There are as many levels of leadership as there are of education. Just because you don't have an M.D., J.D. or Ph.D. doesn't mean you aren't educated. To some, being educated is a GED. To others, it's a Doctorate. Many Doctorates can't lead and many GED's lead multi-million dollar companies.

I have learned that leadership is a process. We all possess varying levels of leadership skills. While some of us are comfortable taking the lead, some of us would rather follow or hide from it, and many of us sway back and forth depending on the situation. At the Academy of Military Science, they believe to be a good leader we need to be a good follower. In essence, to lead well we must be able to hold the vision while staying open to the needs and input of all those around us, staying open to feedback, and maintaining a position of constant learning and growth.

We can all be leaders whether we wash floors, dig ditches, or create the vision and strategies for a multi-million dollar company. Whether we have a title or not, we can all be the leaders in our own lives. The question is what kind of a leader do we want to be and how are we going to achieve this? I asked myself what will it take for me to get through this and operate at my best possible self?

To be a good leader, we need to understand certain aspects of ourselves. Understanding ourselves is like solving a jigsaw puzzle, only we don't get the luxury of the printed picture on the front of the box to guide us. Sometimes, we are not even sure if we have all the right pieces and even if we know we have all the pieces, the thought of starting is completely overwhelming.

Therefore, how do we assess ourselves as being our own leader, and should there be the need to change, how would we do that?

First of all, we have to figure out how we listen to ourselves and how we process what we hear.

Leaders look for solutions and opportunities and tend to be secure in making a decision even if it is the wrong decision because they are decision oriented in their questions and in their thoughts. Non-leaders tend to look to others for decision making, often knowing they may resent it, taking comfort in being able to judge the decision rather than be judged, and tend to be 'stuck' in their ways as well as their thoughts.

In assessing your own leadership skills, concentrate on the following:

- Do you look at what works or what doesn't work?
- Do you look at what you are responsible for or who you can blame?
- Do you ascertain the facts in any given situation or how can you prove you are right?
- Do you assess the big picture or do you protect your turf?
- In each situation, do you examine your choices, or examine how you can be in control?
- In each situation you encounter, do you examine what you can learn or how you might grow, or do you anticipate how you might get hurt or what you might lose?
- In interpersonal relationships do you think about what the other person is feeling, needing, or wanting, or do you wonder what they want from you and why they are so clueless and frustrating?
- Do you think in terms of what is possible or why bother?

You may realize that most leaders would answer the questions listed above with the initial responses, and that all of the 'leader' in us fluctuates back and forth to some degree. Leaders tend to catch themselves in the thought process and switch gears. Many times we don't allow ourselves to do the right thing, albeit switch gears because being in autopilot is easier. This is why people don't usually follow diets, stop smoking, or change their spending patterns. We may "know what is good for us." However, changing our actions starts with changing our thoughts, and our thoughts change with the questions we ask ourselves.

When the question we ask is, "How can I feel better now?" The answer may be a quick fix like eating ice cream, smoking a cigarette, or going shopping. When the question changes to, "What is the best choice I can make for myself right now?" Our answer takes into account all the various things happening in our life and becomes solution-focused, thus increasing our choices, possibilities, and outcomes.

There are more, "I want to's" than there are "motivators to change."

Where do we start and what can we do to build our leadership muscle, the muscle within? Our lives are set by our intentions, and our intentions are set by our thoughts and our questions. Our questions shape our thinking, and our thinking shapes our action. We are trained by our parents and in the formative years by our teachers to believe that 'answers' are good, that some answers are right, that right answers are better, and questions are for those who don't know.

We are pulled, prodded, and lulled into believing that leaders know the answers. In truth, critical thinking is now expected in high school and college, but most of us are unprepared as we weren't taught this in our formative years.

Learning to ask ourselves the right questions in each situation is the first step to bringing out the critical thinker, the leader within. It allows us to become more aware, more intentional, and more effective.

We cannot choose what happens to us. We can only choose what we do with what happens. Leaders choose what they do with what happens to them.

Leaders do not concentrate on the negative. They review their conscious choices and the results they produce.

Again, you don't hear leaders ask, "What's the matter with me? Why am I such a failure? Why are they so stupid? What is the matter with him/her?" Negative questions come in under our radar and usually are not noticed.

Changing your questions come from a place of being open to thoughtful choices and solution-focused thinking, and this gives your leader from within a chance. You will no longer have to remain on automatic pilot. You will begin to develop skills in making conscious and intentional choices rather than being con-trolled by your circumstances. This ability is an essential leadership quality.

Remember, your ability to choose your internal questions puts you in charge of your own thoughts. Your questions provide you the means to think productively rather than reactively. Leading from the inside out starts right here and now with each of us. We have only to ask the right questions.

I asked myself, "Was I going to lead myself in this situation?" Over the loud speaker I heard them call my row number. I got up and walked to the door. My attitude was positive, which is where it would remain over the next several days. I took a deep breath, and headed toward the door with a clear head not led by my fears or assumptions and with the expectations of meeting my challenges with conscious intention, thoughtful choices, positive outcomes and leading from the inside out.

SARAH FERMAN founder of Success Potentials uses her wealth of experience and knowledge in the corporate/business communities and experience as a psychotherapist, so that her clients can connect the dots of their lives and businesses. Her clients as a coach/consultant range from executives, entrepreneurs, professionals, and people in business to the entertainment industry. With Sarah acting as an integrator, clients unleash their potential, activate their strengths, develop strategies to navigate, and build solid foundations to create the successful patterns and less stress in their lives. Sarah can be reached at 1-800-MY-SUCCESS or asksarah@successpotentials.com.

CHAPTER 25

Become the Last, Best Candidate for the Job

CINDRA LEE HENRY

INTERVIEWING FOR A JOB—*one of the top 10 stress inducers. Why?*

Fear, insecurity, and desperation often accompany the job search process even for those who are otherwise savvy and self-confident. To complicate the process, the more rejections the job-seeker receives, the worse this becomes. So what's the solution?

The solution lies in perspective. When interviewing for a job, it's never about you. It's about the employer. It's about what the employer needs and what problem the employer is faced with due to the vacancy in the position they're trying to fill. So, as a candidate you need to shift perspective...stop thinking about yourself and the laundry list of tasks you performed for the last few years. Stop thinking about being nervous or worried that you might not be good enough (or young enough, or any of the "enoughs"). Instead, begin your preparation for the interview process by considering:

- What made it possible for you to excel in your last job?

- What skills did it take to be able to perform your specific job duties?
- What problems does this particular employer need to solve?
- Based on your unique skills set, life experience, and personality how are you uniquely qualified to solve this employer's problem?

While there's much more to this process than what can be discussed in one chapter, this one change in your approach will have a profound impact on your ability to become the last, best candidate for the job. Answering the questions above will serve to set you apart from other candidates and give you a great deal more control during the interview process.

Once you've shifted perspective and explored your uniqueness from the viewpoint of the employer, the next step is to examine the job and the company. Find out as much as possible about both before you get to the interview. Once you're in the interview, it is critical that you discover what the problem is the employer needs to solve. Keep in mind that it's never simply about filling a position. By understanding the problem at hand, you can begin to demonstrate how YOU are uniquely suited to solve it. YOU then become a valuable part of the solution.

The next step in this process is figuring out what possible objections the employer may have to hiring you. The biggest objection I see in my work with older adults in career transition is age. So let's focus on this one particular objection as a way of providing an example of how to prepare for overcoming any objections.

The first question to ask yourself is:
- Why do employers hire the people they do?

The answer to this ultimate question is so simple, so basic, that everyone misses it...including the employer. We're all human—but when we're interviewing for a job it's easy to forget. As human beings the simple fact is, we want to be surrounded by people we're comfortable with. So the simple answer to the ultimate question is...employers hire people they like. But what is it that can cause a person to like someone in the short space of an interview? Well, again, the simple answer is that we like people we're comfortable with and we're comfortable with people we feel we can trust, and we trust people we resonate with, people we relate to because we feel we understand them...and that they understand us.

Therefore, it's never just about whether you have the skills and are capable of doing the job. Of course you have the basic skills necessary to do the job or you wouldn't be applying. So your job as a candidate is to understand the job, the company and the culture well enough to build sufficient rapport so that the employer can "see" you doing the job, so that they "feel" comfortable that you'll be able to adapt and fit in.

Why? Simple human nature and bottom line because:
- We all want to work with people we believe we can get along with.
- The employer is concerned about ALL of their employees and therefore wants to be sure any new person coming into the mix will fit in and not disrupt the team's cohesiveness.
- The employer is concerned about safety and whether the new person will behave in a responsible manner and not jeopardize the safety of others or the safety of merchandise or equipment.
- The employer also wants to feel confident that a new hire won't cost them money through carelessness or undesirable workplace activities.

Given the rationale behind why employers hire those they do, why would an employer care if the next person they hire is over 35 or 45 or 55? First you have to figure out what the fear is behind the objection. What are the fears about older employees? There are typically three:

- **MONEY**. The employer may fear that an older candidate may want more money than what younger employees are already making.
- **FIT**. The employer may fear that an older candidate may not be able to fit in and relate to younger employees.
- **TECHNOLOGY**. The employer may fear that an older candidate doesn't understand the latest technology being used in this job.

So how do you overcome these objections?

First, **MONEY**. Truly, money is just another "fit" issue. If an employer is paying current employees $20, then he can't pay you $40 for doing the same job. Chances are, if you've been in the field for more than 10 years you've probably been making maximum for your position. So when you apply for a new job you may have to take a pay cut. However, salary doesn't end there. It's important to look at all factors related to salary including benefits, work schedule, work environment, commute, and the possibility for career growth. Ask yourself a few questions:

- If you take a job at a lower salary, what are you giving up versus what are you getting?
- Are there ways you can offset a lower income?
- Is it better strategically to be working than not working?
- Can you parlay this job into a better one?
- If you sense some flexibility, is there a way you can prove you're worth more than what's being offered?

- If you were to take this job at the lower salary, could you cause it to evolve into something slightly new and different that would be even more valuable to the employer—something for which you could negotiate a higher salary?

Next, let's tackle the question of ***FIT***. Before going into an interview, if you think age might be an objection, you must ask yourself:

- How well do you relate to younger employees?
- What have you learned from working with younger employees?
- What have younger employees learned from working with you?

Remember, every company has a culture that is the result of the mix of all the employees and the management. If you can't fit in, that culture is disrupted. So, take a careful look at fit from a couple of angles. First, if you harbor resentment toward younger employees for any reason, that resentment will be communicated in your attitudes, verbal communication and body language. No matter how hard you use your intellect to try to create age-friendly responses to interview questions, your true feelings will somehow show. So once again, you must do some soul searching. Find a place within yourself that can understand the true value of a multi-age environment. In my experience, the tangible benefits of blending ages in the workplace include:

- Blending older workers with younger often results in an improved overall work ethic.
- Blending older and younger viewpoints allows for increased openness and understanding and can even out work flow (slow and steady balances quick and sporadic).

- Blending older and younger often results in balance—each picks up something from the other which balances both.
- Age differences can be used effectively to enhance performance, work flow, and efficiency when each capitalizes on their strengths.
- Blending ages causes both to expand their outlook/ perspective.
- This ultimately benefits the customer as well as the employer.

Finally, **TECHNOLOGY**. Let's face it. If you're over 30, you're probably at a disadvantage as far as technology is concerned. But maybe not. First, take a look at how important technology is in the specific job you're applying for. If it is very important, you MUST accept and embrace it if you want to continue in the field. No amount of kicking and screaming will change it.

Think about warehouse workers. In the past this was considered strictly a manual labor job. Now, warehouse workers have to know how to use sophisticated, computerized inventory technology. Not only that, but many of the tasks associated with warehouse work have become automated so human workers may have to understand how to stock, pull, load and unload safely and efficiently as well as how to operate complex robotic equipment. Technology is everywhere. Do whatever it takes to learn it to the best of your ability.

Once you've assessed just how important technology is and have gained an understanding of how it fits into the overall scheme of the company and your job, find out how it complements your unique skills and vice versa. For example in my current job, I use a computerized process for placing orders for customized merchandise. Even though I'm twice the age of the other two people I work with, I learned how to use this particular application quicker and better than either of them.

Why? Well, it certainly wasn't because I am any kind of a computer wiz. It was because I understood the order process from a manual paper trail perspective. They didn't. The manual procedures I'd been accustomed to taught me how to create a computerized system where nothing falls through the cracks and where everything can be double checked, verified and tracked. Thanks to my unique perspective we have cut down on lost orders, miscommunication, and merchandise errors. So the solution:

- Figure out what your strengths are and how your strengths can enhance the application of the technology you'll be using.
- Understand your unique relationship to the technology in order to overcome the employer's possible perception of your potential inadequacy.

Some final words of advice:

Dispel the employer's fear and you have overcome the employer's objection. It's never really about the objection, it's about the employer's fear behind it.

Build trust (which also dispels fear) by allowing the employer to see who you really are. Be yourself but be your best self, the self that is specifically relevant to this job.

Don't use canned phrases; listening to what the interviewer is saying prevents you from wasting their time by repeating empty answers you've found in some how-to book.

Know going into the interview exactly what you want the employer to know about you and then make sure you give them this information in a way they understand. It's your responsibility to make sure the interviewer knows what they need to know about you. They may be good at probing for information or they may not. Don't force the interviewer to pull information from you because they may not bother.

Know why you are uniquely qualified for this particular job. Soul search and spend time figuring out exactly what your value is within the context of this specific job in this specific company. Then practice painting a verbal picture of YOU doing this job, of YOU as the solution.

Finally, be observant. Know as much about this company and the job as you can before going in, then enhance this knowledge through careful observation. Talk to the receptionist before your interview while you're waiting to be called in. It never hurts to be nice to the first people you meet, and the receptionist is usually the first one. Observe activity. See what you can pick up about the company's culture, the climate, the energy, the work flow. Then build this into your interview.

If you follow these suggestions,
you will become

THE LAST, BEST CANDIDATE FOR THE JOB.

For over 10 years I've worked in the staffing industry watching some of the best candidates get passed over for no other reason than that they didn't know how to talk about themselves in an interview. I have made it my mission to help these people learn how to become employed and stay employed making fluid career transitions for a lifetime of satisfying employment. CINDRA LEE HENRY: cindraleehenry@careersinmotion.org, www.careersinmotion.org

⌒

CHAPTER 26

In Business and In Balance™

JENNIFER KALITA

YOUR FIRST ATTEMPTS at balance were frustrating, but ultimately successful. Learning to walk had you stumped, until you figured out having sturdy furniture and supportive adults around to lean on was helpful. You had a goal in sight, and quickly discovered that when you fell, kicking and crying about it brought you no closer to that goal.

Once you had walking mastered, it was time for big girl balance on the see-saw. You began to understand that see-saw success had everything to do with your focus on a give-and-take effort with your teammate, how hard you pushed off the ground with your own two feet, and how centered you kept your body on the board. You also learned how other playmates affected your balance.

While you've walked a million miles since those first steps, and the playground has grown a lot more crowded, what you learned about balance back then still applies. Managing your business while managing your life, and doing both well, feels heavy and hard; the thought of tackling your to-do's and restoring a sense of balance and order makes you feel tired and incompetent.

These feelings are completely natural and more common than you think. But they don't have to stop you from claiming balance in your life. Think about it...when has something scary ever stopped you? Starting your own business felt heavy and hard at times, but you did it anyway. Motherhood made you feel tired and incompetent, but you did it anyway.

There are challenging days when you question your sanity and convince yourself it's only a matter of time until everything that matters comes crashing to the ground. You feel you are just one step ahead of total failure and complete chaos, and you swear as soon as everything slows down, you'll put boundaries in place to steady your pace and enjoy your life.

The good news is that all entrepreneurial women feel this way...often. The bad news is that spring break is not coming. Things aren't going to slow down anytime soon because you, as a powerful woman, are by your very nature going to be out there moving and creating.

The difference between balanced women and *wobbly women* is that balanced women understand and accept that they will at times feel wobbly. Because they have surrendered the fantasy that they will "find time," they have stopped the madness and formulated an action plan to claim the time and the balance they know are possible.

Are you ready to be in business and in balance? Even if you're convinced that stressful chaos is part and parcel of being an entrepreneur, review this action plan anyway.

Decide it. Do you truly want balance? While you may be thinking the answer is a fairly obvious "of course I do," question the truth of this statement. For me, to claim balance was also to relinquish my inner victim. You know her...the "poor me" part of you. We all have her, but I let her run the show for far too long.

I grew up around a lot of drama, and I was very invested in

being a victim for a long time. Being a full-time, easily offended victim, I chose to be around victimized thinkers who couldn't advance themselves or ever just be happy because their negative life perceptions had incapacitated them. You know who I'm talking about; the people in your life who claim nothing is fair and everything is catastrophic. The ugly truth of my connection to these people was that we enabled each other to stay stuck.

If I was going to choose balance, I also had to make a conscious choice to give up my "drama mama." And I loved my drama mama. She made others feel sorry for me. She made people marvel that I accomplished such business success despite all of the unfair personal hardships with which life had plagued me. She made me feel strong that I could walk with such pain and still carry on.

This was, of course, an illusion of strength and I was heavily invested in it. If you are out of balance, then at some level you've chosen it, much like I did. You've avoided boundaries and refused to pull yourself up by your bra straps because perhaps you are committed to the chaos.

At your core, do you really want balance? If the answer is yes, identify three negative patterns that are stopping you. If you can't think of any, ask your spouse or trusted family and friends for critical feedback, with the caveat that you have to respect their honesty and not hold it against them.

Define it. What does balance look like to you? Before you can achieve the peace and order you crave, you first have to define what balance might look like in your life. Is it a cap on your business hours? Does it involve regular self-care? Does it mandate a consistent investment of time and energy in your partner? You have to know where you're going or else you won't know if you've arrived.

Be specific. If balance requires a certain income level or regular involvement in your son's extracurricular activities or consistent volunteer time, put that in the plan. Also, avoid the "not" criteria.

Instead of saying you won't be late for everything, say you'll be five minutes early for everything. Shine a positive light on your balance goals.

Be careful to define your goals for yourself. A friend might tell you to let cleaning or organization around the house "go" and focus on your business. But if you can't get clear in a cluttered space, this other person's definition of balance doesn't work for you and will ultimately render you imbalanced. This has to be *your* definition of balanced living, not someone else's.

Assess what a lack of balance is costing you. How many negative issues in your life are a direct result of being out of balance? If you suffer from chronic stomach problems or regular back pain, remember that these physical ailments are often due entirely to stress.

Think about what this imbalanced approach is costing you in your business. It costs many women the exposure and growth that they're too harried or disorganized to create or pursue. It costs them profit loss, due to financial mistakes and oversights, and often shows up in the form of late fees and missed tax deductions. It compromises their work product or service because they "just need to get it done."

It also costs you the freedom you said you wanted when you started your own business, as well as fulfillment and satisfaction, since you know under the surface you have the power not just to have it all, but to have it all in balance.

Perhaps the greatest cost is the time that's lost with family and friends, because the consequences of imbalance are always on your mind and render you unable to be truly present with the people that matter.

Be honest about the time you have. Like it or not, there are only 112 waking hours per week on average. You can't find time that doesn't exist, so you have to work with what you have if you hope to feel balanced. Not getting clear about this is like putting your bills in a shoebox and then being shocked by late fees and cancellations. If you're trying to cram 200 hours of living into 112 available hours, it's understandable that you're frustrated and out of balance.

Identify your roles. Now that you know how many hours you have to work with, identify the roles through which you spend your time. Most people have approximately five roles. You might be a Self, Wife, Mother, Business Owner, and Volunteer. You might also add Musician, or perhaps that activity falls under Self (if music is a hobby) or Business Owner (if you're a musician by trade).

Create a spreadsheet, or make a color chart on some paper. Track which roles require how much time each day, and you'll soon have a very accurate picture of where your time goes. Color is helpful because you see which colors dominate the chart and whether or not that's a good thing. If you use red to indicate time for your business, and at a glance your time chart looks like a stop sign, *you* need to stop and reassess. "Seeing" the disproportion in this way forces you to confront what needs to change.

Next, make an ideal time chart, illustrating where you want your time to go. This chart will grow and shift, evolving into an accurate picture of the life you want and the life you'll come to have.

Evaluate your support structure. Just as you looked to supportive adults when you learned to walk, and chose balanced see-saw companions, take a look at the people around you. Are they victimized in their thinking? Easily offended and highly self-involved? Is the relationship all give and no take on your part? The people around you have a lot to do with your ability to stay focused, optimistic and balanced.

Or, are you unable to ask for support? If you're afraid people will think you're weak or incompetent if you ask for help, or if you have control issues, think about what that's costing you. Asking for support is a vulnerable experience, but accepting support is a powerful one.

Create action. Create a list of five or more action items you're going to strive for to achieve the balance you want. These may include things like regular exercise or attending two networking events per month to grow your prospect base. Incorporate one item per week.

These may also include items of inaction. Perhaps you're taking on too many clients because you fear a lack of future income. If you take on too much work at one time, you can under-perform and thereby level your long-term business goals.

Find an accountability partner. Ask a trusted friend or colleague you respect to meet with you at specific intervals to discuss your progress, or hire a coach if you're concerned about objectivity. Your accountability partner must be respectfully honest with you, so avoid your best friend or assistant, since they may be hesitant to tell you what you need to hear.

Remember that balance is a choice. Getting clear about the time you have and making informed decisions about commitments in your life and in your work will enable you to live in balance and therefore in abundance.

Look into this downtime you've been hearing so much about. Learn to put prospects on a waiting list. Empower your children by showing them a woman in consistent harmony—not a woman in perpetual crisis.

Take action to create a life that's in business and in balance. You really can have both.

JENNIFER KALITA has been a communications and business consultant, writer, speaker and strategist for more than a decade. She empowers entrepreneurs to live a life In Business and In Balance™, and has educated thousands of entrepreneurs in all facets of business launch, development, and promotion. She is the founder and CEO of The Kalita Group (www.thekalitagroup.com) and Strategic Women (www.strategicwomen.com); Boomer Buzz PR columnist at Second50Years.com; and author of numerous books and business development programs.

CHAPTER 27

Tell Me YOUR Story

LYNNE KLIPPEL

IN 2001, I had it made. I had a terrific job doing work I loved. My boss and I were on great terms; very close friends and collaborators. We built a program from scratch to serve troubled teens and had plans to expand it mightily. I was in line for big promotions and planned to work in this setting for at least 20 more years.

Then, the bottom of my world fell out. In the space of 30 days, my job was gone, the program closed, and my boss left town in disgrace.

Six years later, I can now see that losing that job was the best thing that ever happened to me. My life is infinitely better today than back then.

That story tells you something about me doesn't it?

Stories have the power to connect us, inspire us, teach us, and help us make more money. In fact, prestigious institutions teach seminars on the power of story in business. This article will explore the power of stories and present some ideas on how to use stories to increase your network and your net worth.

People today are overwhelmed. We are bombarded by advertisements, ezines, time limited offers and a glut of information. We are also more isolated than past generations. We live further away from family members, have less time for friendship, and spend more time with machines. We hunger for a human connection with someone we trust who will just tell us what to do.

Stories link us. While factual information touches our minds, stories touch our hearts; bonding us, creating motivation, energy, and enthusiasm. By sharing our stories and listening to the stories of others, we reduce our feelings of isolation and overwhelm.

I was scared to death. It way my first seminar, and I felt like a duck out of water. I didn't know a soul. Everyone seemed so much more successful and intelligent than I was.

At the first lunch break, a kind woman invited me to join her group for lunch. She told me about herself. Then, she got out some paper, a pen and interviewed me. She asked me all sorts of questions about my life and my business. She was such a good listener that I felt comfortable being myself. When I finished my story, she asked me how she could help me build my business.

I'd just received my first lesson in networking from a master.

Forming relationships is one of the most powerful ways to build a business and increase profits. Yet, we rush from networking meeting to networking meeting, collecting business cards by the dozen, then entering the information into elaborate contact management systems. We are disappointed when we see little results from all that hard work.

However, networking isn't about quantity, it is about quality. Successful business people will tell you that relationships which lead to referrals and contracts are generally not formed in a five minute encounter at a meeting. The strongest business relationships are based on mutual respect combined with an understanding of who the other person is and what skills they bring to the table. Collecting stories from the people you meet will begin the basis of a strong and enduring business relationship.

I belong to two networking groups. One is very traditional in format, with set times for passing business cards and asking for leads. The other group is very non-traditional. Each meeting has forced random seating so you are always sitting by someone new. At the beginning of each event, a question is asked of the group, which enables participants to share a story from their life.

Last month at the first group, I collected three business cards from interesting people. At the second group, I heard an incredible story about how a very successful realtor used to take her baby to work when she was nursing in the 1960's. Another woman shared about the pain of losing her mother and how focusing on her business helped cope with her grief.

Research tells us that women in particular bond with each other by sharing our wounds as well as our joy. When we take a risk and share our stories of overcoming a challenge, we show our listeners that we trust them. More importantly, we communicate that we can be trusted to listen and honor their stories of challenge and triumph as well. If you want to create a feeling of community in a relationship or a group, the best way to do so is to give people opportunities to share their stories in a safe setting.

However, you have to be prudent and wise about which stories you share, especially in a business setting. The goal of your stories should be to share part of your self, not brag about your children, your accomplishment, or your trials. Have you ever met someone who tops every story you tell with one that is better? The kind of person who believes that if your clients are challenging, hers are worse? If your labor lasted 10 hours, hers was 35, etc. This form of competition is damaging to relationships.

Another pitfall is sharing stories that are too personal in nature, too early in the relationship. When someone shares an intensely personal story, the listener can feel uncomfortable. For example, I once interviewed a woman for a job who spent the bulk of the interview telling me about her horrible marriage. It was a great story, but the wrong place to share it.

The other mistake some people make is to tell stories that are not true or are embellished. When you meet someone who tells you a story that doesn't ring true, you are automatically cautious around that person. In fact, you will probably avoid them like the plague and never consider them as a business partner or vendor. If your story is not authentic, people wonder if you are someone they can trust.

I once interviewed an industry superstar. She had it all: wealth, fame, beauty, notoriety, and a great family life. She was so successful that she had to turn clients away even after she raised her fees to $500 per hour.

I almost fell out of my chair when she told me she still worries about money. She shared her fears, left over from the early days of her business, that she would not be able to meet her monthly expenses. Then, she laughed and told me that facing those fears and not letting them get in the way was an essential task for all successful people.

Her story gave me hope. If someone at her level of success still occasionally worries about money, I'm not such a loser when I fight my feelings of lack. What a relief!

Listening to stories from successful people motivates you, inspires you, and gives you the information you need to create success. Yet, you don't have to be at guru status to share your story. Many people would rather hear a success story from someone who is just a bit ahead of them on the road to success instead of already at the finish line of success. When someone asks you about your story, don't be afraid that you don't know enough to share it. Share what you know, your heartfelt experiences, and watch your relationships deepen and your business grow.

Are you ready to increase your network and build strong business relationships? Use these tips to incorporate storytelling and story collecting into your professional life and watch it begin to blossom:

- Everyone you meet has a story to tell. Strive to collect a story along with each business card.
- Ask open-ended questions that invite sharing like, "What prompted you to start your business?" or "Tell me a little about your favorite customer."
- Listen intently, maintaining good eye contact.
- Keep the focus on the other person, not on you. Avoid trying to top her story with one of yours.
- If asked, share one of your stories. Make it real, honest, and heart-centered. Your real story will inspire others, regardless if it is a story of triumph or of a challenge.
- Close the conversation with a bonding question like, "How can I help you build your business?" or "What kind of people should I refer to you?"
- Surround yourself with successful women who are willing to share their stories. Look for books, radio shows, and live events where you can connect. Give yourself a regular diet of motivating stories to keep your enthusiasm strong.

When you start purposely collecting and sharing stories, you will not only grow your business, you will increase your enjoyment of life. You'll have more friends and cherish all the new relationships that develop.

And then, when our paths cross, I'll be waiting to hear your story too!

LYNNE KLIPPEL hosts an internet radio show, which celebrates the real stories of women with successful businesses: www.Web SororityTalkRadio.com. An author, speaker, teacher, and popular coach, Lynne loves to help women make their dreams come true. She resides in the Midwest with her husband, three sons, and a houseful of pets. To learn more about Lynne and listen to her free radio show, visit www.LynneKlippel.com

CHAPTER 28

Turn Your Small Business into a Brand-Name Success

JENNIFER McCAY

DOES THIS SOUND like your work day?

You stay on the phone, frantically trying to make a difficult client happy, attempt to stay on top of the tax issues you face as a small business owner, perhaps also worry about a nagging personal matter such as a sick child or how you can manage to take time to do something for yourself for a change. And that huge stack of work you've saved for a rainy day looms large because there's no rain in sight.

In the midst of all of this, you still haven't even *begun* to find the time to market your small business—no small feat since it's the only way you can get enough clients to afford to pay the bills. You're already dreading the calm that follows the storm of work that you're handling right now. You might even question why you wanted to go out on your own to begin with because it's hard to pull things together.

Was that an accurate description of a day in your life? Does the mere thought of taking the time to promote your business stress you out? If so, keep reading.

PUT AN END TO YOUR PROFESSIONAL "DEAD ZONE"

Instead of thinking about all the hustle and bustle, imagine for a moment that you no longer have to worry about getting the word out about your business, that people call you more often than you have to pursue them. That the fear you currently feel about the "dead zone"—the time when you don't get as much business as you would like—disappeared long ago, never to return.

How is this possible? How could you start achieving the kind of small business success that you always wanted? By turning your small business into a brand to be reckoned with.

What's a brand? I like to think of it this way: When you think of Oprah, Madonna or a Volvo, you immediately have an image in mind, don't you?

Oprah Winfrey is a strong, bold woman who succeeds using her own mix of confidence, opinions and common sense. In case you're either not from the U.S. or have lived under a rock for the past decade, Oprah is *the* most successful female media professional. *Forbes* ranked her as the number one celebrity in 2005, as well as the ninth most powerful woman in the U.S. When the name "Oprah" is spoken, people listen.

Madonna is the eternal chameleon who will never stop impressing audiences with what she's come up with this time. Like it or not, she is an icon—and a well-branded one at that.

Volvos own the "safety" brand. If you want a car secure enough to keep your loved ones safe and sound no matter what, you know that a Volvo is the very best because the company has been so consistent in using safety as their key brand concept for dozens of years. They've cornered the market using a very basic message.

See how just saying the name "Volvo" gives you an instant feeling? Same with "Madonna" or "Disney" or any number of other well-branded household names. You immediately grasp what's being discussed and have a sense of what the company or individual stands for. More than likely you have an emotional response to that brand the moment you simply hear the name.

By creating a brand—a consistent image of how your business is perceived—you, too, can harness the power that these famous people and companies have in your own market niche.

WHAT IMPRESSIONS HAVE TO DO WITH YOUR SUCCESS

Have you ever met a professional organizer whose car was full of clutter? Have you ever had a colleague introduce you to someone "you just have to meet" whose zipper was undone at a professional meeting? These sound like obvious mistakes that are easily swept under the rug from a social standpoint, but professionally speaking, they're brand suicide. In fact, both of these real-life scenarios indicate the power of first impressions.

We don't like to think of ourselves as judgmental, but in truth, we all make snap decisions about the people we meet. Frightening but true, every time a potential client encounters anything to do with your business (including yourself), an image sears itself into your prospect's brain just like a branding iron sears its way into cowhide—good or bad.

Thankfully you can literally use your brand to make the right impression every time (though you still must remember to zip up!) —showing your prospects that you have the competence, skill, expertise in your field and trustworthiness they need to send you their hard-earned money.

DON'T JUST GET THE WORD OUT.
BECOME A BRAND-NAME EXPERT

To brand your business effectively, first you need to recognize that you are an expert in your field and embrace it as an undeniable fact! It never ceases to amaze me how common it is to hear highly talented people just like you say they aren't experts at what they do—possibly because we all know someone in our line of work who's been doing it longer, but most likely it's because we're afraid to sound like we're bragging.

Here's the insider's scoop: You cannot wait for someone else to dub you an expert—you must reach out and grab the title!

If you don't, you will more than likely continue to suffer the frustration, overwhelm and panic that rule every business day when you're not getting the right kind of attention for your business on an ongoing basis.

Besides, it's not bragging if it's true. Once you do something professionally for a period of time, you end up learning a *lot* more than the average person who requires your products or services. You know what to look out for and have the ability to give others guidance. In other words, compared to laypeople who purchase from you, you truly *are* an expert. So shout out your status as a well-branded expert to the world. Soon others will chime in, so you won't have to as loudly!

DOES YOUR CURRENT MARKETING MESSAGE PASS THE HIGH-CONCEPT BRAND™ TEST?

At Avenue East, we specialize in helping our clients develop High-Concept Brands™ for their businesses. Unlike most branding agencies, we don't just recommend you hire a designer to develop a fancy logo and call that miniscule means of showing off your corporate identity a brand. A logo is not a brand and never will be. (Your brand must project from the inside out and is much more than a logo, which is only a visual way of communicating your brand to others.)

Instead, the idea of "High-Concept" came from the movies. The folks in Hollywood are always on the lookout for movie ideas that are special, instantly understandable and appeal to a specific target group. When they find an idea that can be explained in a sentence or less, they call that winning script "High-Concept."

When you create a way of referring to your business that gives an instant positive impression to your ideal clients, has appeal for the right people and can be implemented in every aspect of your business, that's your High-Concept Brand™. It is emotional, powerful and has a human touch.

Such a clear definition makes it a snap for your prospects and clients to turn to you when they need what you offer. The simpler the concept, the better. And if your High-Concept Brand™ has a little of the "wow" factor—well, achieving success in your business just got a lot easier.

Instead of feeling panicked about where your next client will come from, take action now to articulate exactly what it is about your business that is special:

- Think about why your current clients come to you and which characteristics of your business are advantageous for clients and prospects alike.
- List all the emotional reasons why your prospects might be frustrated if they give their business to another vendor instead of you, as well as why they will be happier coming to you.
- Name the details about your business and your personal expertise that set your business apart.
- Analyze your target audience. Is your niche sufficiently narrow so that you can speak directly to your prospects' specific needs in all of your business communications?
- Write down all the ways in which your clients and prospects encounter your business, from promotional items, business cards, how you answer the phone and everything in between.

Once you have answered these questions, you will begin to see ways in which you can articulate your small business brand in a way that passes the High-Concept test with flying colors. Before long, the pain of never having enough business will be long gone, and your business will begin to skyrocket. Isn't it time you branded your business?

⌒

After spending years helping clients such as Sony Europe and Adobe with their brand communications, today JENNIFER McCAY helps small business owners like you succeed. Her step-by-step guide, The High-Concept Brand Bible™: Think Big, Find Your Focus and Achieve Small Business Success, shows you how to brand your business using effective big business strategies scaled down for your needs and budget. Get all the details, as well as free weekly marketing lessons at www.avenueeast.com

⌒

CHAPTER 29

If You Build It, They Will Come

LIZ PABON

FOR YEARS WE HAVE heard about the power of attraction—the Law of Attraction to be exact. Whether we are interested in attracting a new romantic partner, or a new client, the law of attraction states that the energy we vibrate—what we focus on—attracts others with a similar vibration. The challenge is that we often know what we want but aren't clear how to attract those amazing opportunities so that they come to us instead of having to chase after them.

Personal Branding is a process that enables us to create the shift in mindset needed to ignite the Law of Attraction. This may come as a surprise considering that branding focuses on the experience one has with your brand. Well, in the world of Personal Branding, creating an experience that connects your target audience to you is the ultimate end-result. But how do we get there?

BREAKING GROUND

Like any well planned construction development, Personal

Branding begins by digging deep to unearth the real YOU. Your ultimate success in attracting the right opportunities starts by being clear on who you are, what you stand for and your overall distinction.

Because we are unaccustomed to looking at ourselves so intimately as it relates to our business, this process is foreign to us. Many of the marketing tactics we implement in our business are based on an outside-in approach. Logos, marketing collateral, and spiffy copy do not a Personal Brand make.

Personal Branding, on the other hand, is strictly an inside job. The process employs a strategic approach that asks you to have a heart-to-heart with yourself answering questions like:

- What do I value most?
- What are my greatest talents?
- What am I most passionate about?
- What am I praised for?
- How do others see me?
- Where do I see myself in the next 6 months, 12 months, 24 months, etc?

Uncovering what is at the core of who you are and what makes you tick will provide you with a clear picture of your unique brand attributes and help you begin to shape your brand statement—what defines your brand.

Think of the Personal Brand development process like building a home. You must first break ground before you lay the foundation and construct the home. Remember the story of *The Three Little Pigs*? The only home the wolf was unable to blow down was the home built with brick because it was the sturdiest.

Your Personal Brand, once identified, developed, and nurtured is unshakable and is what will ultimately attract opportunities to you. The next time you wonder what you can do in your business to make a memorable impression, consider showing your target market a little more of you!

WHO'S ON YOUR GUEST LIST?

So, once your Personal Brand is developed and is as strong as a brick house, you are ready to dig into your target audience.

The most enjoyable parties are those in which not only is the food great, but the company is even better. Careful consideration goes into planning the guest list to ensure that enough "like-minded" people are in attendance and that a unique mix of characters are invited to keep everyone engaged.

When you think about your target audience, do you give as much consideration to the mix of players as you do when planning a fantastic party? If not, don't worry. You can always make today the day you look at your target audience differently!

Some of the most powerful Personal Brands do an amazing job of connecting with their audience because they are not only clear on the power of their own brand but know precisely who they want to connect with. They have determined their most perfect fit.

Oprah, for example, is not only clear on her brand values, but she has also identified a specific group of women—her primary audience—with a passion to "live their best lives." Personal development, professional development and giving back, are just a few of her target audience core attributes.

As it turns out, Oprah's target audience is comprised of women just like her! The next time you watch her television show, take a look at the audience. It's been said that the Oprah show draws some of the most attractive audience members who, coincidently, don't look that much different than Oprah herself.

Several years ago, when I launched my own business, I began the process of identifying my target audience and determined that my ideal and primary market is professional women not unlike me. I developed my "Ideal Client Profile" and discovered that my values and long-term goals aren't that different from those of my target audience.

Ask yourself:
- What does my ideal client look like (inside and out)?
- What does my ideal client value most?
- How does my ideal client spend their free time?
- Who do I wish to work with?

Much like a fantastic party, when we match our unique Personal Brand with that of our ideal target market, sparks fly. Communicating to this audience happens with greater ease because we are now not only able to quickly identify them upon first meeting, but they are able to identify us as well. This is the magic that occurs when the Law of Attraction is ignited.

LOOK WHO SHOWED UP!

Connecting to the brand called YOU places you and your business in motion in a way you never thought possible. Your well-defined brand provides you with clarity in who you are, what you stand for, who you wish to connect with and why. Armed with this realization, you are able to communicate your brand at all touch points that are right for your brand (Yes, you'll now know how to invest your time, where and with whom). Essentially, you will possess a super-charged persona that makes you unstoppable. You'll not only attract abundance for yourself, but you will encourage the best in others.

WHAT YOU THINK ABOUT, YOU BRING ABOUT

Being clear on the brand called YOU and those attributes that make you unique means you become keenly aware of those attributes. This suggests that you will begin to notice these attributes in others. Have you ever noticed when you prepare to buy a new car and decide on a make and model you suddenly see that car everywhere? That's attraction in action. The Law of Attraction states that what you think about and focus on, you bring about in your life. So, if you concentrate on more abundance, success and contentment you will attract those things for yourself. Additionally, if you wish greatness for others, you will attract those things for you as well—the ideal win-win situation.

WHAT GOES IN MUST COME OUT

It is not uncommon to think and speak from a place of lack when things aren't going our way. Considering how the Law of Attraction works, if you possess a mindset of lack, you will attract lack. So, the next time you are tempted to say or think about a need, instead think and talk about those incredible brand attributes that you possess. Instead of saying or thinking, "I need to have at least three more contracts this month to make ends meet," try something like "My ability to quickly put people at ease is bringing me more than enough clients this month." Get the idea? Placing your focus back on the strengths of your brand will ensure that you attract those positive proclamations in your life.

YOUR PRESENCE SHOWS OTHERS THEIR POTENTIAL

Is your Personal Brand centered on creativity? If so, and you focus your attention on that creativity, you will create an energy field of creativity around you that attracts other creative types and encourages others to tap into their own creativity. The result is a feeling of being empowered by being around you—you now become a magnet for creativity.

Are you beginning to see the Law of Attraction does not work alone? In order to activate the Law of Attraction, you must unlock the door to its power. This power is unlocked with a key you possess through your Personal Brand. Failing to identify and tend to your Personal Brand does not allow your greatness to flourish, and your ability to touch the lives of others will never see the light of day.

In our hands, we each hold a tremendous amount of power. Tapping into this power requires a shift in our mindset. Once we ignite the power within us, we can then focus on those attributes that make us unique, distinctive, unlike anyone else. It is then, and only then, that we unlock the door to the Law of Attraction and benefit from its wisdom.

We no longer need to struggle for the opportunities we seek. Instead, with Personal Brand in hand, and heart, we will attract those opportunities and jump off the small business merry-go-round to a place where success is abundant and appears with greater ease.

ENJOY THE JOURNEY!

LIZ PABON, "The Branding Maven," is inspiring, motivating and empowering—but most importantly, she's effective. A speaker and author on the topic of personal branding, Liz delivers insights and principles that are proven to achieve WILD SUCCESS. Liz publishes the weekly Keys 2 Wild Success! ezine. If you're ready to ATTRACT amazing clients, set yourself APART from the pack, make a lot more MONEY, and have a lot more FUN in your small business, get Liz's FREE WEEKLY TIPS by going NOW to www.thebrandingmaven.com!

CHAPTER 30

A Dollar and a Dream

LINDA ARLENE SCHWARTZ

"Anything you vividly imagine, ardently desire,
sincerely believe and enthusiastically act upon
must inevitably come to pass."
—W. CLEMENT STONE

IN NEW YORK CITY they say, "All you need is a dollar and a dream." And you, too, can become a millionaire if you win the lottery. In my case, the odds of achieving my dream were just slightly more realistic.

Even though I am neither fond of games nor gambling, I must admit that I do enjoy taking risks with my life. Big ones. In poker it is said, "If all you have is a chip and a chair you're still in the game." For me it was just a matter of showing up—me, my massage table, and my invisible friends. Call them angels, spirit guides, advisors, or dead friends. Whatever. Even the massage table itself was a gift from a kind stranger who happened to be the manager of a friend's building I was visiting. Apparently, a former tenant had left it behind and the manager felt inclined to offer it to me.

YOU ARE ENOUGH

It was the mid-80's—a prosperous time for some people. I was not one of them—yet. I had about fifty dollars in my pocket and 75 cents for a subway token. My assets included some defaulted student loans and a mountain of personal debt.

Yet, I was bound and determined to make it in New York City. I realize that most people don't start a business on a negative budget, but that was all I had. That was what I did. Nothing was going to stop me. I just believed!

CONTRAST INSPIRES MOTIVATION

I forgot to tell you why I came to New York in the first place. I love music and the arts. But I was sick and tired of hearing pedestrian lyrics that sounded like mantras to a lesser God—the God of bad relationships and limited thinking. I was so disgusted by the abundance of violent and uninspiring films that I got it into my head that somehow I could make a difference. Despite my debt, student loans and bad credit, I was going to change the world. Ha!

By the time I landed in Manhattan I had a very good idea of what I didn't want to be when I grew up. Having exhausted every possible career and fantasy job from travel agent to bookseller to high school teacher to social worker to psychic healer, past life therapist, channel and massage therapist, I was crystal clear about my life purpose and market niche. (A corporate job was obviously not among them.)

CLARITY OF PURPOSE AND CONGRUENCY

A wonderful book, *You Can Have it All* by Arnold Patent, Esq., provided the clarity for my one line purpose statement: "To use my intuition and communication skills to inspire, inform, and entertain, such that people might happily choose to express the highest octave of themselves, particularly those in music and film."

I wanted to inhabit a world of inspired art forms and dedicate myself to their proliferation. Since I already had a long history working at the grassroots level of non-profits and the public sector—the reason for my current impecunious state—I now asked the Universe, God or whoever was listening whether I might now have greater influence working with leaders. Based on my history, this was a long shot!

Nevertheless, my prayers were soon answered in a manner uniquely characteristic of my Candide-like journey. I began having visitations by spirit guides who had been leaders in their prior incarnations. After recovering from the initial shock, I conferred with colleagues to determine that I had not finally gone off the deep end. I finally surrendered to the crash course that those guides were graciously offering me—the energy management of high-powered individuals—both those 'in body' as well as 'out-of-body.'

> *"When you want something, all the universe*
> *conspires to help you achieve it..."*
> —PAULO COELHO, from *The Alchemist*

For several months I was rigorously coached and encouraged to immerse myself in the reality I wished to create—consultant, advisor, healer of those in the arts—someone whose services were in high demand. I was even given a client roster. I had to 'act as if' despite the appearances of my exceedingly humble circumstances! Talk about a stretch! While I was living hand-to-mouth on the sofas of friends, colleagues, and acquaintances, I concurrently had to hold the vision and vibration of the new life to which I was giving birth!

This all pre-dated the movie *Ghost*, and I will say that some of the assignments given to me by my new spirit guides were so outrageous—even to me—that I was extremely fortunate to have a team of dear colleagues to verify the accuracy of my perceptions, so I knew I wasn't going mad! Rather, I was becoming more and more attuned to subtler vibrations...It was an exciting yet frightening time!

Before *Ghost Whisperer* and *Medium,* I was directed to convey messages from the Great Beyond. YIKES!

DELUSION OR PERSISTENCE?

I wondered many times whether I was delusional . It was no surprise that many friends later confessed their concern that my angels might finally abandon me in this latest venture. However, when one ponders the situations of others who have succeeded in a big way, the question arises: What differentiates delusion from great success? I believe it is persistence...

Ray Bradbury was a mediocre high school student who dreamed of becoming a well-known author. He sold newspapers on a street corner during the Depression while maintaining his daily writing schedule. Jim Carrey wrote himself a million dollar check while envisioning a brilliant career with no demonstrable evidence it would ever happen.

LIVE YOUR DREAM NO MATTER WHAT THE APPEARANCE

While I was becoming "healer to the stars" in my mind, I was also rolling pennies and doing whatever it took to survive. I did impromptu readings, healings, and treatments anywhere, anytime with anyone who asked and some who didn't...paid or unpaid.. From conversations with cab drivers struggling at their day job, to fellow straphangers riding on the subway to strangers drinking mimosas at Le Relais (a trendy boite), I was simply in service to humanity.

CELEBRATE ABUNDANCE IN THE SCARCITY

One of the most valuable coping skills I learned was from June and Jim Spencer, the authors of *No Bad Feelings*. It was the technique of finding abundance in every situation rather than playing tug-of-war resisting scarcity. I was to surrender to it, embrace it, befriend it, and finally celebrate it! WHEW! That was a tall order yet a huge breakthrough!

As a result, I became the local expert in finding the best breakfast deal of either a bagel and egg sandwich or the largest bran muffin, both including coffee. For the grand total of $1.25 they stuck to one's ribs for the rest of the day!

Sometimes our most severe challenges can be transformed into the greatest blessings. After so many years of insistence upon my 'champagne taste on a beer budget' I can gratefully say that resourcefulness has become one of my strongest attributes.

JUST TAKE THE LEAP

At a certain moment I grew tired of struggling and paying my dues. I gave myself a year to make it or break it in New York. I quit my day job at a high school and used the final pay check to attend a music industry conference. I threw bread on the water and offered generous comp sessions to prospective clients. A few responded, but they were the right few.

Twenty years later I am still receiving referrals from those initial comp sessions. I never advertised. I had no website. I wanted no press. I just wanted to create a safe, private, discreet, and sacred environment for those working with Muse and Inspiration.

A space in which they might transform, doing what they loved and what I loved.

While it is true that my client roster read like a "Who's Who" of the entertainment industry and people wondered how that happened, I knew it was always about love. I had written a precise client profile that I constantly updated. I asked to have those led to me with whom the connection would be mutually uplifting. My policy was that I would only see clients I loved, whether funds were ever exchanged or not.

Some still think that the power of love is just another spiritual platitude. But in fact that is not the case. It is a higher frequency vibration that moves more quickly and efficiently through the density of third dimensional reality. Living at a higher, more loving vibration magnetizes you to those on a similar plane...and just makes good business sense.

Did I really make a difference in that world after all? I would like to think I did, though sometimes when I see the current trailers I do wonder. As for the next adventure, she said to herself, "If you don't like what you see and hear, write your own damned music and screenplays!" So she did...

LINDA ARLENE SCHWARTZ has been on a conscious spiritual path since the age of 12. As an Intuitive Coach, Transformational Bodyworker and Spiritual Advisor, she incorporates humor, irreverence, and intimacy with Spirit in order to initiate breakthroughs and to inspire you to be the most of who you are. Her focus is on the practical application of spiritual principles to daily life. She has over 20 years experience working with leaders in the arts, entertainment, and industry . She is also a songwriter and storyteller. You may reach her at Arlayne22@aol or www.lifereadingbodyworks.com

PART III

SPIRITUAL FULFILLMENT

CHAPTER 31

The Voice Within

RAVEN APONTE

IN 2001, THREE DAYS AFTER September 11, I found myself in a small boutique-style beauty parlor in Mission Viejo, California, with 12 other attendees of a workshop being held by Dr. Vernon Woolf. Dr. Woolf is a behavioral psychologist with a background in Quantum Physics who was teaching a workshop on a method he calls Holodynamics. What had just transpired days before was lingering in the minds of us all, and I remember feeling there was a special reason why I was there with my husband and some of our dearest friends for this workshop we had registered for weeks prior to 9-11.

Looking back on it however, I realize I had no idea what a profound exercise I would be introduced to that day. It is this exercise I wish to introduce you to, so you can explore the possibilities of achieving the success that myself and many clients over the years have experienced. This exercise is one that has taught me how to tune in to my Full Potential Self and access the part of me that is all-knowing, all-wise, all-loving, and completely free of limiting beliefs and fears. I learned that day that my Full Potential Self was connected to the Infinite Intelligence, also known as the Quantum Field, and that I could engage it and communicate with it at will to access the information in that field. Since that pivotal weekend in my life, I continue to access my Full Potential Self daily in meditation and have received incredible guidance from this part of my self in all areas of my life.

The reason Dr. Woolf calls this part of us our Full Potential Self lies in the discoveries of Quantum Physics. We are all made up of energy. What Quantum Physics has discovered is that all energy has the same "full potential" or "maximum potential." They've discovered the smallest unit of energy that can be measured has the same "maximum" or "full" potential as the energy of the entire universe.

Before I share with you the simple steps of the exercise I use to access my Full Potential Self, I want to share with you the importance of accessing this part of yourself on a regular basis. I am going to solicit the assistance of a brilliant author, Napoleon Hill, and his classic book, *Think and Grow Rich*. I recently came across some incredible citations from one of the later chapters in the book. The story of how I came about reading this information is worth mentioning here because it has a mystical quality to it that for me was nothing short of Divine!

I was meditating and tuning in to my Full Potential Self, when I was guided to read the chapter in *Think and Grow Rich* that was about sexual transmutation. I thought this was interesting, because I remembered that when I had read, and even re-read the book, I'd always "skimmed" over that chapter, which is actually entitled "The Mystery of Sex Transmutation." Upon reflection, I think the whole idea of somehow mixing "growing rich" with something "sexual" bothered me subconsciously. However, receiving this message in my meditation, I found my copy (it wasn't far away and if you haven't read it I strongly recommend that you do), and I re-read this chapter, this time fully engaged. In it, I found some incredible information that was in perfect synchronicity with my desire to find a way to introduce this concept to people with the help of credible resources.

I was amazed at what I was reading in this book written in 1937. It detailed a similar practice to that which I was taught by Dr. Woolf in 2001! It was fascinating to be reading his accounts about people such as Abraham Lincoln, Thomas Edison, Napoleon Bonaparte, William Shakespeare, Edgar Allen Poe, and many others, "tuning in" to what I believe Dr. Woolf would call their Full Potential Self for guidance.

In agreement with what Dr. Woolf taught us about connecting to our Full Potential Self in the workshop, Napoleon Hill talks about the importance of developing what he calls your "Sixth Sense." He says:

The sixth sense is creative imagination. The faculty of creative imagination is one which the majority of people never use during an entire lifetime, and if used at all, it usually happens by mere accident...The faculty of creative imagination is the direct link between the finite mind of man and Infinite Intelligence. All so-called revelations, referred to in the realm of religion, and all discoveries of basic or new principles in the field of invention, take place through the faculty of creative imagination.

He encourages us to develop this faculty of our creative imagination and says:

The creative faculty becomes more alert and receptive to factors originating outside of the individual's subconscious mind, the more this faculty is used, and the more the individual relies upon it and makes demands upon it for thought impulses. This faculty can be cultivated and developed only through its use.

The great artists, writers, musicians, and poets become great because they acquire the habit of relying upon the "still small voice" which speaks from within, through the faculty of creative imagination.

Hill then goes on to tell the true life story of an inventor named Dr. Elmer R. Gates who had a "personal communication room" that was practically sound proof and all light could be shut out. He details how the doctor would go and "sit for ideas," during which time he would use his creative faculty to access the Infinite Intelligence for ideas. Corporations would even hire him to "sit for ideas" for them.

It was amazing to be reading this stuff in this chapter after practicing a method of using my own "creative faculty," or accessing my Full Potential Self, for many years. As I was reading about the practice of Dr. Gates of "sitting for ideas," I kept seeing myself in some of my favorite meditation spots where I actively access my Full Potential Self and "sit for ideas" daily. The fact that it was during one of these "sittings" or meditations that my Full Potential Self guided me to read that particular chapter was a gift to let me know I am on the right track and to share these words with others. As Napoleon Hill says:

A relatively small number of people use, with deliberation and purpose aforethought, the faculty of creative imagination. Those who use this faculty voluntarily, and with understanding of its functions, are geniuses.

ACCESSING YOUR FULL POTENTIAL SELF
TO UNLOCK THE GENIUS IN YOU!

As promised, below are the steps for accessing your Full Potential Self.

HOW TO ACCESS YOUR FULL POTENTIAL SELF

Step 1. Find a quiet place to be and get comfortable.

Step 2. Close your eyes and go to a PLACE OF PEACE in your mind. Simply imagine yourself in a peaceful place and see yourself there in your mind's eye or imagination.

Step 3. Invite your Full Potential Self to join you in your Place of Peace. Say to yourself silently, "I invite my Full Potential Self to join me in this place." Your Full Potential Self is that connection that you have to the Infinite Intelligence. It is all-loving and all-wise and knows exactly who it is. It will recognize that you are calling on it. (I've never had a client be unable to connect to this part of themselves by using this exercise.)

When you invite your Full Potential Self to join you in your place of peace, there are many different experiences that can be had or felt. In your mind's eye, you may see someone or something joining you in your place of peace. You may just have a feeling or a sense, or a vibrational shift. Just be open to whatever you feel.

Also, try not to get caught up on the language. If you're not comfortable asking your "Full Potential Self" to join you, feel free to use a different name to call this part of yourself. For example, some call it their "Higher Self." The important thing is that you know that this is the part of yourself that is connected to the Infinite Intelligence.

Step 4. Once you feel or see your Full Potential Self join you in your Place of Peace, you can ask any questions you may have or ask for guidance or advice on any situation. The more you practice, the more you will learn to discern when your mind is answering you and when you are truly tuning into the Infinite Mind or Infinite Intelligence.

Step 5. GO FOR IT and ENJOY!

Repeat steps 1-5 as often as possible. Connecting to this part of yourself is truly the way to unlock your own genius from the voice within!

RAVEN APONTE is a Certified Life Transformation Specialist, helping people uncover and transform the hidden fears and beliefs that are limiting their potential. She has her degree in Psychology from U.C. Berkeley and is a Certified Facilitator of Holodynamics. If reading this chapter piqued your interest, and you would like to experience freedom from the limitations that block you from living your highest potential, please visit www.magicaltransformations.com or call 1-877-MINDSET to sign up for a free consultation.

CHAPTER 32

Beyond the Mind:
Moving Into
the Power of Be-ing
DANIELA BUMANN

"To Mind or Not to Mind…That is the Question"

A WAY INTO "PRESENT" BEING

WE ARE ALL HUMAN beings, not human doings. It is for this very reason, that I believe in the process of moving beyond the mind into a state of "BEING." This is where true vitality and peace of mind are experienced. One of the easiest ways to get out of your head is to get into your body by increasing your awareness, creating life balance, and connecting your "inner landscape" to your outer world. This process is really quite simple once a daily momentum has been established, yet it seems to elude many of us because we try to *go there* predominantly with our mind. Seduced by the preoccupation and zest of doing, the peace and clarity that increased being brings often escapes us.

A recent session with a client illustrates this dilemma very clearly. In the beginning stages of increasing awareness, the intellect with its incessant questioning can exhaust the presence and peace that could "be" there otherwise. Having just shared several intense 'happenings' of her life experience, my client stopped her mental process for a moment, looked up at me and awaited my response. I briefly shared with her some ways in which she could—just be— with her situation and feel her way into presence "allowing for her greater wisdom to come in." Immediately she exclaimed, "Yeah, but how do I "do" that? How do I "DO" that?"

And there goes the age old dilemma of BEING vs. doing—HOW DO I DO THAT?—Funny isn't it? Our preoccupation with doing has depleted many of us and left us dry on a mental, physical, emotional and even a spiritual level. Certainly a balance is required between both, but as a general rule, the more you are being yourself, the more the doing will flow naturally and effortlessly.

ENGAGING THE ART OF "BEING"

BEING by nature is SIMPLE. It is not elaborate, or fussy. It just asks you to be real—to be 'true' to you. Can you be that? Can you be with that part of you that simply is, but doesn't do—yet through its very alertness and presence 'creates' and vibrates into manifestations, beyond anything you could have 'done'?

Interestingly, but not surprisingly, as I was getting ready to engage in the writing of this chapter, all sorts of information 'popped' in. Lovingly assisting me, reminding me to BE even more with this experience and the topic at hand, helping me to juice up and match up with what was most ready to come forth.

"Being" at its most basic is the ability to be 'fully' present inside your body. Fully inhabiting it, and not just occasionally glimpsing at it, becoming a *full time* resident not a *part time* occupant. Why not befriend your very own 'Temple' by treating yourself to look at its beauty in a loving embrace? Your body is your very own host to your mind and spirit all in ONE. As your inner strength and body awareness is building, you too are growing in your own "Presence" Power and Stamina.

Learning how to pay attention to "HOW YOU FEEL" and to stay in touch with how your body reacts to your life creations—i.e., the people and things in it, has the great ability to keep you *here* in touch with what is 'true' to you in this moment! This process of paying attention builds a lovely bridge, connecting you again into 'present being.' Maintaining and staying connected to your inner core of strength and stamina facilitates a more grounded, centered and solid state of being, truly cultivating living from the inside out.

Delightfully, whether I am teaching at a conference, coaching an individual or a couple, their experience in varying degrees always remains the same! As I am guiding them through their body and into "the presence of their being," the response is felt! Having had their awareness brought 'back' into the Body... there is a palpable shift of energy in the air. A Space—a stillness is created where "peace" of mind reigns supreme! A release of something held so tightly, is suddenly let loose.

Directing our attention back into the Body has the amazing quality of bringing it 'all together' and making us feel whole again. This place of no judgment is not excluding anything, but including everything in Body, Mind and Spirit. All One, whereby empowering us by allowing us to experience the Peace/ease and Joy of being.

I think many of us have heard the saying: "There is no such thing as the present moment." Yet even though we know this, we pursue the next second, oblivious to the fragrance and the richness of the moment past. Knowing has never gotten us rooted into being, because being is not something you DO or know. It is the very essence of WHO you are.

HOW PRACTICAL IS ALL THIS?

Imagine—if you are not as present in "this" moment as possible, where exactly are you, and how does that affect the health, quality and effectiveness of where you currently are? Think about it...This flows, spills over into every area of your life, enriching or impoverishing it. This impacts all of your relating, whether to yourself, in your personal relationships, career, or your passion and purpose of sharing your mission and gifts with the rest of the world.

At this very moment you may feel yourself stretched to the 'max' and pulled in different directions. You may be feeling scattered and not quite sure what you are grounded in. I invite you to expand your ability to just "BE" present with what is, as it is for just a moment. Relax, and take a deep breath into your belly down into your toes. Just trust that by being more fully, you will be able to BE, DO, and HAVE anything you choose to. Ultimately, whatever brings you back to your 'senses' is your divine right in guiding you to experience heaven on earth.

TAPPING INTO THE "POWER OF BEING"

One of *Vibrant Living's* CREATIVE MOVEMENT PROCESSES™
"S* I* M* P* L* E*"
for GREATER FOCUS, CLARITY AND GROUNDING:

First, it's important to ground yourself in feeling that, "*being is at the Heart of all you're doing.*"

WRITE this Process down in full, along with each step separately, on an index card. Next DECIDE what you need most, and from here set the stage. Remember to FEEL your way through it. Create a 'relaxed' sacred space for you to feel, reflect and literally move through the steps. Another method is to just pick one of the 'cards' created and go from there. Whatever you do, have FUN! 'Immerse' yourself in being SIMPLE and creative.

- **SIMPLIFY:** Keep 'it' easy and simple, unobstructed, don't be allured by glitz and glitter, and don't make mountains out of mole hills. Keep your emotions in check, proceeding with clarity. **KEY:** Slow things down so you can really see; Move into more Silence.
- **IN -TUNE:** Intuit the next step; feel your way through it 'balancing' heart with head, stay 'tuned in' vs. tuned out… you know what to be-do. **KEY:** Stay 'in tune' with what feels right to you— Trust and follow your Insights/Inspirations leading you along the way.
- **MOVE:** Move your body from head to toe; engage your innate rhythm, moving to grounding in your 'own' inner drummer. Experience and expand your sense/ory awareness; really taste, touch and feel your life. Take it 'in'; don't just let or give it out! Move your body and feel the joy of being in sync. **KEY:** Amp up you Sensory Awareness, Move and Dance, Make Love, Sense your surroundings. Enjoy Nature and Animals.
- **PAY ATTENTION:** To what and whom is affecting you; is it life giving or draining? BE present and alert to 'your' life's creations, choices and unfolding. Watch your dreams/commitments. Are they fulfilling or depleting YOU or serving someone else's dream? Be alert to supposed obligations. **KEY:** Stay on 'Your' path! How do you FEEL—pain or pleasure? PLAY!
- **LAUGH:** It's just a 'life situation,' but not your whole life! Infuse a 'true' sense of humor in this Game called Life. PLAY at it! Look at the children engrossed in play, as it is their 'real' life. You may get it all done, and you may not. But if you have not laughed a lot, hugged, giggled and gone silly while making love, what have you done? **KEY:** RELAX & CHILL and let your life in!

- **EXPERIENCE:** Be open to 'Experiencing' and keep OPENING to this most wondrous, mysterious process called life! You can and will not figure it all out. But I promise, if you continue to allow love in, let hurt out, embrace and release resistance to your 'greatest' good, your Adventure will be an amazing one; your spine will be chilled with excitement and maybe, too 'incredible' even for you to believe. **KEY:** OPEN TO EXPERIENCE TRUST & BELIEF!

DANIELA BUMANN is the Founder of "Vibrant Living" and the Creative Movement Process™. She is a Swiss native, and received her degree in Movement/Dance Therapy form the Guggenbuehl Institute in Basel, Switzerland. As a life, movement and wellness coach she has been teaching and guiding people of all ages and walks of life for over 15 years to find 'true' confidence and self realization. Daniela is a certified seminar leader, speaker and facilitator seen on Showtime television, showcasing the Vibrant Living process™. Please contact her at: www.movementwithjoy.com or (888)753-5884 for a FREE consultation.

⌒

CHAPTER 33

Your Body is Telling You Something:
Are You Listening?

TARNIE FULLNOON

STRESSED? TIRED? DEPRESSED? Tight neck and shoulders? Get headaches, backaches, a painful hip, or some kind of body symptom? Pain and body symptoms are the way your body speaks to you. They indicate something is out of balance. These body messages usually start subtly at first, however if ignored, they get stronger and stronger until they scream at us through pain, illness, disease, emotional imbalance or mental distress. Too often our body pain and symptoms get way out of balance before we act. Then we seek medication, doctors, tests, healing supplements, and spend too much time and money trying to find a cure. What if you had a way of listening to your body so you could really give it what it needs?

The simple fact of the matter is our body is full of information for us. We just need to listen to it! We need to learn techniques to translate our body's language. Our body has a great capacity to heal itself, however most of us abandon our bodies on a consistent basis and don't stop long enough to feel the sensations or listen to what it is trying to tell us.

Are you ready to listen to what your body has to say, to listen more deeply? In this chapter you will be given exercises you can use by yourself or in conjunction with a health practitioner to assist you in supporting your body's communication towards health and healing.

When the connection to ourselves is interrupted, and we don't have access to our inner dialogue, our body will produce symptoms and pain. When we are blocking our body's feelings and sensations, we are stopping the line of communication within ourselves. We are unable to use our body symptoms and pain as a vehicle for healing. To suppress our feelings we use drugs, alcohol, nicotine, sugar, food, sexual promiscuity and sexual inhibition. We get caught in excessive thinking or captured by our feelings and stay in anger, fear, anxiety, depression, shame. Our body tenses, we feel unfulfilled and alone, and suffer in pain and discomfort physically, mentally, emotionally and spiritually.

Our body communicates to us through body symptoms and pain. It wants us to listen to it, to hear it, to feel what it has to say. It is vital for our health, well being and healing to do this. *A client of mine was struggling with increasing weight from sitting at a computer all day. She expressed how she had "contracted" into her mind and forgotten her body. She came to me because she was starting to have health issues which included losing her balance. When asked to take a deep breath and spend some time inside herself, she said she was numb inside and felt guilty for spending time on herself.*

If I asked you how you felt in your body *now* what would you say? Try it. What are you aware of?

We are conditioned in this world to be doing, producing, taking care of someone else, making money, often moving in automatic response to life. It is our unconscious response to our conditioning to focus on the outer world and not include ourselves. Taking time to feel yourself, feeling into your body symptoms and pain means stopping, and spending time going within. This will often bring out judging and critical voices that say "this is a waste of time" or "you should be doing something else". What our body needs is for us to reprogram this negative self-talk.

So how do you become more acquainted with your body? How do you take time for yourself to listen to and connect with what the body symptoms and pain have to share? Here are four simple exercises to use:

• **Awareness of Breath**

Exercise: Take time to breathe into your body, where is your breath going? Does it reach your toes, your pelvis, your chest? As you breathe ask yourself, "What do I feel? What am I aware of inside?" Become conscious of your breathing often during the day.

• **Attention Inside your Body**

Exercise: Close your eyes, focus your attention on your breath inside your body, allowing the feelings and sensations that are present to come forward. Have a sense of seeing or touching yourself from the inside. The purpose is to feel your body just the way it is; don't try to change anything. Spend five minutes each morning and evening with this exercise and repeat it daily until it feels like something you "want" to do for yourself and your body!

• **Movement of the Body**

Exercise: Put on some gentle, flowing music. Get comfortable standing. Take your breath and attention into your tailbone. Breathe into the spaces around it, above it, below it, inside of it. Begin to move your tailbone, spending some time doing this. Then with your tailbone leading, begin to move your spine like a slow moving snake or a piece of seaweed, feeling your spine unwinding. Continue this for at least five minutes. This movement deeply connects you into your body.

When I take my attention and breath inside and move, I have access to all my sensations and feelings, I am deeply in my body, I lose my inhibitions, my fear; I move into a state of no-mind. I unwind the tightness and contractions that have built up in my daily life. I reconnect to my inner being, my soul, to my authentic Self; I feel calmer, more present, and trusting of my own rhythm and needs.

It is important to note that when we start re-inhabiting our body, we open the doorway to what we have avoided or repressed. You might experience a flood of thoughts, feelings and images; you might feel tense or uncomfortable, or you might feel nothing. Allow whatever comes up to be OK and do not fight it. Know that it takes courage and commitment to connect inside, especially when you are just beginning.

• Focus on Body Symptom or Pain

Exercise: Have some soft music playing, and a pad and colored pens ready. Take your attention and breath inside, focusing on your chosen pain or body symptom. Breathe into the spaces around the area, gently, without forcing. Easily and softly move the area just like you did your tailbone and your spine from the previous exercise. When you feel you have connected with the area (you might find images, sensations, colors, words, feelings emerge), stop moving and select a colored pen. Write what you experienced. Don't hold back.

When you are done, bring your attention back to the area you were moving and focusing on. Ask it, "What do you want or need?" Pick another color and respond. The key here is to use the color to assist you in separating out this part of your body and allow it some airtime. What is it trying to say, what does this body part want you to know?

Another client came in with a shoulder injury from a rock-climbing incident. Treatment included physical healing associated with the shoulder and neck. Also included was the movement and dialogue work as described above. The shoulder pain became a gateway into her body's feelings and sensations, allowing deep healing to occur and revealed more of her authentic self. What emerged was how numb and disconnected she was; how she used food to stop feeling; how sexually repressed she was, and underneath she found a history of sexual abuse from her father. She has now returned to rock climbing, is leaving her corporate job and doing something she has always wanted to do- mural painting.

I use these exercises consistently in my personal and professional life. It assists me in my own healing, staying present, listening to my body, and moving forward on my consciousness path. The key is to do it consistently and make it a habit! Do it regardless of what your mind is saying and the excuses you have, and choose yourself daily, being open to what is revealed. It takes conscious practice to bring our attention back to ourselves and to listen to what our bodies have to say, and it is well worth it in the end. You will radiate your aliveness!

All the great teachers have guided us to spend time by ourselves. When we experience the joy of being connected to ourselves, it becomes like eating delicious food, or exquisite lovemaking. We feel the YES! of life vibrate through our body. Our mind talk changes from "I should...I need to" to "I get to...I want to."

A retired professor client of mine once told me if she could listen and take care of her body like she takes care of her house (car, job, children, others), she would be in wonderful shape!

Are you willing to give yourself the gift of listening to your body? Our body is a magnificent creation! It holds our life story: who we are, how we feel, and what we think. It is an expression of our consciousness and a powerful tool for gathering and giving out information. I encourage you to use it! You deserve it!

TARNIE FULLOON is an Australian trained Physiotherapist with 26 years of experience, including owning a successful sports injury practice in Sydney and serving as a PT for the 2000 Olympics. Combining her traditional training, her own self-healing work, and a Masters in Spiritual Psychology, she has created BodyFreedom: a mind-body physical therapy practice. Besides her private practice, she runs classes, workshops and does speaking engagements. Visit: www.bodyfreedom.com, e-mail: tarnie@bodyfreedom.com or phone: (626) 296-2032

CHAPTER 34

Emotional Alchemy

DR. MEG HAWORTH, Ph.D.

EVERY THOUGHT YOU THINK has an emotion tied to it. This is true whether you are aware of the emotion or not. Everything you do or say begins with a thought. This very book was created first as a thought. It then became manifest into concrete reality through many motivated people who made it happen. Every thought that went into the production had a feeling attached to it—excitement, joy, elation, frustration, worry, caring, fear—there were a myriad of emotions that created this very book in your hands that right now you are reading, thinking and feeling all at once.

As a person dedicated to self improvement, you have learned about the power of your thoughts. You have discovered the power of thinking in a positive way. Conversely, you have learned how negative thinking can bring yourself and others around you down. You may have also discovered that no matter how positive you try to think, negative emotions will always come up. What if these negative emotions weren't such bad things? What if they were actually in place to teach us something about who we are? What if we welcomed them with the same eagerness we have for positive emotions? What if these negative emotions actually held the key to our healing?

Emotional Alchemy is a process that helps you identify the emotion that is running the show and keeping you blocked. You get to see how and why the emotion is in place, how to release it, and how to bring in what you truly desire. It acts like a computer system that helps you erase old programs you no longer need. You then get to load on new programs to boost your energy and overall well being. You can use this process as many times as you like for all time. You become the healer of you as you participate in your transformation.

Begin to think of your negative emotions as teaching emotions. They are here for a reason, and it's not to make your life worse. It's not to trip you up or punish you in any way. We live in a world of duality. Because of that, we will always have the experience of up and down, back and forth, happy and sad. To deem negative emotions as bad or wrong only places judgment and undue pressure on a perfectly normal part of our existence. To pretend they do not exist is to ignore half of you, and this part of you may very well bring the gift you are looking for. Emotional Alchemy assists you in learning what your teaching emotions have come to share with you. When you choose to listen to and learn from your teaching emotions, you open up to the possibility of clarity, self-under-standing and inner peace.

Simply thinking in a positive way is not enough. It is also important to feel the emotion of the positive thought you are thinking. If you do not feel the feeling behind it, you will be unconscious of what is fueling the thought. Think of your emotions as having an electrical current that determines the outcome of any given situation in your life. For instance, if you think the thought, "I am financially abundant" but you do not feel the truth of it, you will probably remain in the same financial situation you have always been in and wonder why the affirmations you have been using have not been working. You must have the positive current of the emotion coupled with the thought in place to secure the positive outcome. If there is no movement in a particular area, a teaching emotion may be present, and its negative current may be canceling out the positive current of your thought.

To give you a deeper idea of the importance of your thoughts and feelings, consider that your thoughts may be a function of your personality, and your feelings may be a function of your soul. Also consider that you are here to evolve through a partnership between your personality and your soul. Think of your soul as the great teacher and your personality as the student. The soul teaches you through your experiences and your reactions to those experiences. The personality chooses to participate in the assignments given by the soul or not. Just like in school, if you don't pay attention, do your homework, pass the tests and learn, you will fail the class. If you feel like you fail a lot or in some areas of your life, then all your personality has to do is change how it is choosing to participate in the lessons that are being presented. Emotional Alchemy offers a way for you to participate, learn, pass your tests and move on to the next phase of your learning and evolution.

The word Alchemy, as defined by *Webster's New World Dictionary* is ". . . any magical power or process of transmuting a common substance, usually of little value, into a substance of great value." Emotional Alchemy takes the less valued negative emotion, learns from it, releases it, then replaces it with an emotion of great value.

THE PROCESS

Begin by identifying what the immediate problem or issue is. For instance, you may be upset about your business not doing as well as you intended. Then move to step one.

1. The Madness—this is what you feel about the problem. Make a list.

   > I feel afraid
   > I feel confused
   > I feel like a failure
   > I feel unworthy
   > I feel disappointed

   Choose the emotion that has the most charge for you from the list. 'Disappointment' (this is the emotion you will be working with).

2. Close your eyes, take three deep breaths then scan your body for any tightness, soreness or discomfort. If you have more than one place, concentrate on the physical sensation that is the loudest.

   'Your throat is tight'—the disappointment is in your throat. You will do the work there.

3. Ask the following questions of the emotion (disappointment)
   a. Why are you here?—listen for the answer.
   b. What role do you play in my life?
   c. How do you affect me?
   d. Am I willing to let this go?
   e. Feel free to ask other questions that may lead you to insights about the emotion. Get creative and allow the flow of information to occur.

   After you receive an emphatic "yes" to releasing the emotion then proceed.

4. The letting go or self forgiveness process:
    a. Focus on your heart to feel the most loving, caring part of you. Envision your heart self-traveling to the throat (or other physical location you are working in.) If you are a visual person, it may be helpful to you to imagine what your heart self and the emotion might look like. Let your imagination create the form they take.
    b. Feel the heart self-give love to the emotion, feel it change through love. If you have a hard time receiving the love, double the love current. Keep at it. When it feels filled up with the energy of love, proceed to the next step.
    c. Feel the emotion being pulled out of the throat then sent upwards into light for transformation.
    d. Notice the difference in the throat when the emotion is gone.
    e. Replace the newly emptied space with the positive emotion of your choice. Joy, for instance. Then envision something that brings you joy like dancing on the beach. See it happening in the place in the body where you were working.

When you have completed the process, take time to feel the difference in your body, mind and Spirit. Notice the change and appreciate what you have done for yourself. Go down the list if you like and release each emotion you identified at the beginning.

Go at your own pace and be gentle with yourself if you feel you do not get it right away. When you wake up to a new perception, possibility or process, it takes time, attention and practice to implement. Give yourself the time you need. You can also try this with a partner who wants to support you in your growth. Having an ally in your healing can be a huge help.

There is a gap between who you think you are and who you know you are. For some this gap is very wide. For others it is a step or two. No matter how wide the gap, your emotional self will always hold the key to your transformation. The current of feeling is the foundation for your life path and purpose. Your excitement and passion is just as important as your fear and sorrow. When we are blocked by feelings that seem to hurt or hinder, we are typically being provided with an opportunity for deep and meaningful insight and healing. Let your feelings be your guide and allow Emotional Alchemy to show you who you've always known you are. You are always in the process of becoming who you are. Feel deeply, love fully and be who you are.

DR. MEG HAWORTH, PH.D. helps people dramatically transform their lives through Transpersonal Psychology (Spiritual Psychotherapy). Currently in private practice in Los Angeles, Dr. Meg is a nationally known speaker, teacher, writer and practitioner of holistic healing. If you are in spiritual crisis, need assistance with a block, have received all you can from traditional psychotherapy, or desire guidance and direction, call for a free 30 minute telephone session. drmeghaworth@aol.com , www.doctormeg.com, (626) 483-0214.

CHAPTER 35

5 Secrets to Ecstatic Living and Being All You Can Be

DIANA DIVINE LIGHT, MA, DD

WHEN WE WERE CHILDREN, anything was possible. A stick magically became a sword, and in a heartbeat, we were fighting a dragon or Darth Vader. A colorful cloth became a skirt, and we were dancing and swirling in delight. Immediately, our child's imagination took us on a magical journey.

Our most amazing gift is our imagination. One man's imagination, Walt Disney, created Disneyland, an amusement park filled with imaginative experiences and fast moving rides. While another man, John F. Kennedy, held a vision for a nation that resulted in taking us to the moon. As adults, anything is still possible, with vision and imagination. Having and executing a clear plan insures that what we imagine will become a reality. Here are some secrets I have learned to ensure Ecstatic Living.

First Secret: Go inside and ask, "What do I want?" and "What don't I want?"

The First Secret is to go inside and ask yourself, "What do I want?" and "What don't I want?" This does not have to be difficult.

Be willing to play with this and let it be easy. Think of it as though you were playing as a child would play, fully engaged in the magic of discovery.

Next create two lists. On the first sheet of paper write what you want "more of" in your life. On the second sheet of paper write what you want "less of" in your life. Just keep writing, for several days if need be, until the "Ah-ha's" start coming up. An "Ah-ha" can be a sigh, an idea, or a flash of knowing. An "Ah-ha" is the place that brings you new insights about yourself or a situation.

The reason for writing what you don't want is to help you dig deep and become more clear on what you do want. Bringing more of what you do want into your life and less of what you don't want will bring more aliveness and ecstatic living into every area of your life.

Second Secret: "Tell the Universe WHAT you want and WHEN you want it."

After you have two rather lengthy lists, take the "what you want" list, go through it item by item and write down in present tense, what you "want" and "when" you want it. Perhaps you want to be happier. Write: "I am happier now."

Perhaps you want money. Write: "I am rich, each and every moment."

Perhaps you want deeper connection in your life. Write: "I am deeply connected to the Love within me, to the Love within others and to the Love of the Divine, every moment I breathe."

The Second Secret is to "Tell the Universe WHAT you want and WHEN you want it." The Universe is neutral. What we put out, we get back. If we say, we want to be happier, the Universe says, "yes" to us, especially if we tell the Universe "when" we want what we want.

It is our job to tell the Universe WHAT we want and WHEN we want it. It is the Universe's job to provide the HOW it happens and WHO comes into our lives to help make it happen. For example, when I say, "I am rich now," my imagination begins imagining all the ways I am rich. The Universe then mirrors what I am putting into it by bringing me opportunities to become even richer. It brings me rich people to emulate. It brings me ideas, which will help me become even richer.

Third Secret: "Listen."

The Third Secret is magical. We have clearly told the Universe "what" we want and "when" we want it. Now it is time to "Listen." What do we listen to? We listen to everything that helps direct us to what we want. Let's say I have declared, "I am happier now" and I am 50 pounds overweight. By listening to everything...I am also listening to my body, my deeper needs, my joy and what would make me happy. I go to eat another donut, and I notice a voice within that says to me, "What would REALLY make you happier in the long run? You don't have to eat this one. Play some music you like, dance and drink water instead." I listen. I make a different choice. I choose to REALLY make myself happier on a deeper level. I turn up the music and dance. Immediately, "I am happier, now." I am bringing "what" I want into reality.

I have begun Micro Listening. Micro Listening is when I hear more than what my stomach wants. I hear my stomach wants the donut, and at the same time, I hear my "happiness quotient" wants me to be deeply happy in the long run, so I skip the donut and deepen into what will REALLY, deeply make me happier. Now I can choose my happiness, because my "listening" has included a choice I didn't know I had.

Fourth Secret: "Act."

The Fourth Secret is to act on what you hear and wait until the "why" becomes revealed to you. Recently, I was traveling in Guatemala. It was around Easter time and I had taken a fluffy bright yellow chick (stuffed animal) with me that was wearing a hat of blue and white checked bunny ears, tied on carefully, under the Chickie's chin. It was so adorable. I called it Chickie Bunny. Well this day, Chickie Bunny didn't want to ride in my backpack any more, so I put her in the front seat on the dashboard. (I listened and acted.)

As we headed back across the border into Belize, my girlfriend, who had the map, told me to take the next turn. I did. (I listened and acted.) We followed the road quite a while, until I realized it didn't look familiar. It was time to check and see if we were going the right way. It was time to ask someone for directions.

I pulled over and there was a woman sitting at a table mixing something that looked like tortillas in a bowl. Her bright eyed, long dark-haired daughter was playing close by. Her husband was standing by the table. I showed them the map and where we wanted to go. After much discussion, he in Spanish and me in English, it was clear we were on the wrong road and going the wrong way.

When I got back in the car, I looked at Chickie Bunny. I knew Chickie Bunny wanted to be with the little girl. (I listened to my knowing and acted.) I grabbed Chickie Bunny, walked over to the family and kneeled down. The little girl came running to me. I handed her Chickie Bunny. Her eyes shone like sparkling black diamonds. Her face lit up like the Fourth of July. Excitedly, she ran to her Mother, who I could see had tears of joy in her eyes, while her Father stood with his chest out, smiling proudly through his broken teeth. They stood in joy and wonder, looking at Chickie Bunny sitting on their rough-hewn wooden table.

Fifth Secret: "Be grateful for everything that comes your way."

When I climbed back in the car, my friend said, "As long as I live, I will never forget those faces and the joy radiating from them." I realized, I had stayed in joy and gratitude, even though I had made a "wrong" turn. I even thought later, perhaps Chickie

Bunny might have had a secret agenda! She wanted to be with that child! Something drove me there. Something inspired me to give that beautiful child Chickie Bunny. My inner child likes to think Chickie Bunny secretly arranged it, and I was wise enough to listen and act.

I could have been upset for making a wrong turn and wasting time. Instead, I chose to stay in gratitude in the moment and listen to my inner deepest counsel. I chose to act on that listening. It was after I acted, in faith, that I got the "why" of my actions.

Being grateful for those things that please you is not enough. By being grateful for everything that happens to you, whether you like it or not, changes your "happiness quotient" dramatically. I got to experience the joy of Being All I Can Be.

The 5 Secrets to Ecstatic Living and Being All You Can Be can be summed up as follows. First, be clear on what you do and do not want more of in your life. Second, create a "what" and "when" to all that you want. Third, listen to everything that brings you closer to what you want. Fourth, act on your inner listening. Fifth, be grateful for everything that comes your way. Being in joy and gratitude for whatever happens in your life is the most amazing way to Be All You Can Be.

DIANA DIVINE LIGHT is the Founder of an International Network of Individuals, www.GlobalMastersNetwork.com, who know they are Masters and support each other in their Mastery of all Life Skills. Diana, is multi-talented in Healing, (Graduate of Barbara Brennan Healing Science), facilitating Sacred Circles, Tantric Dance and inspiring others to "Be All They Can Be." Please email her at DianaDeLight@cox.net or call her at (949) 551-8191 to set up a Global Masters Network near you.

CHAPTER 36

You Are Already Enlightened

REV. KATIE PEPE

You are already enlightened.

I WAS A YOUNG MOM caring for three babies in diapers when I read that in a book. Harried and exhausted, I was searching for God. A lifelong devotion to the God I met in Catholic Mass and Holy Communion vanished. I went to Mass and prayed for God to appear there, but I heard only words, dry words, empty words washing over me. Still I was harried and searching for God.

One sound rose up from this parched litany and continued to reverberate, over and over within me: I Am. I Am. I Am. The I Am was like an inner voice beckoning me to be still and stop searching. I obeyed and realized that what I was searching for outside of me was inside of me, as near as my beating heart. Regularly sitting in silent meditation over the past fifteen years, I discovered the I Am presence within me.

It's within you too, because you are already enlightened.

The I Am presence shines within each living being like the sun.

Just as dark clouds sometimes block the sun's brilliance, our negativity can overshadow our enlightenment. Spiritual practice is the work of releasing negativity to reveal the enlightened One within.

This One has many names: In Hinduism it is the Atman, Infinite center of every life, in Buddhism it is known as Buddha Nature, while in Christianity this perfection is referred to as Christ Consciousness. We aren't born Buddhist or Christian; we inherit our faith traditions from our ancestors. Rather than blindly rejecting or embracing this legacy, a mature world citizen can step back and imagine the God's eye view of the world, and find their own unique place within it.

Picture all of earth's God-seekers praying in their own traditions: legions of Jewish men in synagogues wrapped in prayer shawls swaying as they recite the Torah each morning and evening; millions of Muslims prostrating themselves five times each day facing Mecca; countless monks and nuns chanting the holy office in the middle of the night, while Sufis dressed in white whirl and dance their prayers.

Rather than a cacophony of discordant sounds, the beauty of diverse spiritual expression creates a majestic Interfaith symphony, which beckons all to join the dance, sing the songs, and recite from sacred text.

Interfaith spirituality honors the sacredness of all paths to enlightenment. It embraces the wisdom of the saints and sages throughout time, while cultivating a living, growing spiritual practice to reduce obstacles and reveal the enlightened I Am presence within.

INTERFAITH INSPIRATION:
FIVE STEPS TO REVEAL YOUR ENLIGHTENED NATURE

Begin Where You Are:
Honor and respect the religious training of your youth and use it as a stepping-stone to a mature and fulfilling spiritual life. I dis-

covered a Christian method of meditation called Centering Prayer, which was an introduction to a fulfilling spiritual practice within my inherited religion.

When I began studying yoga and eastern philosophy several years later, I recognized that while methods and philosophies vary, the experience and benefits of spiritual practice are similar.

Observing spiritual practitioners from a variety of disciplines, I concluded that the benefits were enjoyed by all regardless of the method. I witnessed myself and others gradually release dysfunctional habits and attitudes that had been severely limiting and excruciatingly painful. I watched people forgive what seemed unforgivable, and reap the rewards of liberation and joy which radiated from faces wiped clean of suffering.

If your religion is not fostering spiritual growth or has caused you pain, acknowledge your feelings and release the past. Begin anew by seeking a wider, Interfaith approach. Remember that institutionalized religions have been organized by humans so they're subject to the same limitations as their organizers. Glean the essential wisdom which resonates with your heart and let go of the rest.

Commune Daily with Your Christ Consciousness, Atman, Buddha Nature:

Enlightened thoughts and actions are nourished by daily spiritual practice. By focusing on your I Am presence each day, your awareness of it increases while negativity and suffering begin naturally to dissolve in the bright light of your pure spiritual nature.

To reveal your Buddha nature, feed yourself like the Buddha on a healthy daily diet of inspiration, meditation, and prayer. A junk diet of gossip, negativity, and trashy entertainment feeds the lowest common denominator of human nature and obscures Christ Consciousness. Be discerning about what you ingest. Starve negativity in yourself and others by refraining from gossip, judgment, and hurtful speech.

Most people complain there's no time for daily spiritual practice. The busier you are, the more you need it. You'll soon discover that with daily spiritual practice, you'll accomplish more with less effort, because your mind becomes calmer and your emotions less distracting. Often times, the people you live or work with will notice positive changes in you first. My young children noticed I was calm and happy after meditation, and soon learned to tiptoe quietly outside my room when I prayed.

Choose a time and place for your spiritual practice and stay faithful to your intention. Set up an altar in your home or office as a visual reminder to focus on your commitment to liberate your spiritual nature. Arrange icons, pictures of holy people who inspire you and sacred text in a pleasing way. Include candles and fresh flowers to entice you to spend quiet time morning and evening nourishing your enlightened self through prayer, chant, or study.

Detoxify Your Body and Your Home:

Your body is the temple of your spirit. This majestic temple is bombarded daily by toxic chemicals in food, water, personal care and cleaning products. The last century on planet earth has ushered in a host of synthetic chemicals which negatively impact our minds, bodies, and spirits. Our elegantly designed human bodies were never meant to withstand so many unnatural, harmful substances.

Detoxifying and simplifying your life as a spiritual practice is extremely healing. It's a loving act of devotion which creates a serene and balanced home for your spirit and aligns you with the highest good for the earth. Your enlightened spirit shines brighter through a healthy body, so care for it lovingly and be sure to rest, exercise and drink plenty of pure water.

Begin to reduce your exposure to toxins by choosing healthy, whole, organic foods when possible. Reduce or eliminate your use of caffeine, nicotine, alcohol, and drugs. Replace personal care products and household cleaners with natural, non-toxic alternatives.

Adopt a Worldview that Embraces Learning:
If you value learning and transformation, you're less likely to judge yourself and others. We're all works in progress. If you can accept yourself and others as learning, evolving and growing, you release the heavy burden of perfection and righteousness. Most of us, however, have a strong attachment to being right.

I remember complaining bitterly to my spiritual mentor about some grievous wrong committed upon me by another. How passionately I wanted her to agree with my righteousness and condemn this other, who was so obviously wrong and hurting me. After exhausting myself listing all of this other person's glaring flaws, Mary asked with an impish grin, "My darling girl, would you rather be right or be free?"

The beliefs and opinions you hold dictate your words and actions. If you believe, for example, that you must defend yourself or launch a counterattack when someone criticizes or insults you, you are trapped in a dance of negativity led by them. You may be right, but you're not free. Loosening your grip on the need to be right will set you free to respond in new ways, perhaps metaphorically placing a flower in their rifle barrel and dancing away.

Buddhist teaching refers to this principle as beginner's mind, a receptive attitude which seeks understanding and acceptance rather than the narrow measures of right and wrong or good and bad. The Buddhist saying goes, "In the mind of the beginner, there are infinite possibilities; in the mind of the expert, there are few."

As a beginner, you bring a fresh perspective to everyone and everything. When you embrace the belief that we're all here learning to transform our personalities to reveal our enlightened goodness, it's much easier to accept and forgive ourselves and others. We wouldn't scold a baby who falls many times while learning to walk. Each of us is learning to walk in our glory and is bound to fall repeatedly.

Practice Wu Wei:

Wu Wei is a Taoist philosophy of spiritual discernment and simplicity. When you are aligned with your enlightened nature, action arises spontaneously, effectively, and effortlessly. In the Taoist sacred text, *The Tao Te Ching*, Wu Wei is defined simply: "The way to do is to be." It predicates doing upon being. Learning to connect with the elemental flow of the Universe leads to inspired action which is graceful, easy and joyful.

The *The Tao Te Ching*, asks in Chapter 15: "Do you have the patience to wait till your mud settles and the water is clear? Can you remain unmoving until the right action arises?"

When life's muddy challenges demand enlightened action, pray to be shown what would contribute most to the highest good of all concerned. Trust that there's a win-win solution to every conflict or challenge. When you don't know what to do, do nothing. Take a deep breath. Ask for Divine guidance. Wait patiently for your intuition and "gut feelings" to lead you to right action which serves the highest good of all concerned.

In our shrinking global village threatened with violence and destruction, there is an urgent need for enlightened citizens committed to right action. Together we'll birth a peaceful planet when the spark of enlightenment is liberated in all people. Then, perhaps, we'll greet one another as the Hindus do, with the word, *Namasté* which can be translated as "The Divine in me bows to the Divine in you."

Namasté

REV. KATIE PEPE is an ordained Interfaith Minister. Her work is inspired by the timely message of the Interfaith Movement, which honors all paths to God as sacred. Her writing, teaching, and counseling embody the essence of inspired religious teaching, adapted for today's spiritual seeker. She performs inspiring and unique ceremonies for all of life's milestones. She can be reached at (551) 482-0801 or katiepepe@aol.com

CHAPTER 37

Healing the Hole
in the Heart/Soul

JOY SANDERS, AHP

OUR SEXUAL ENERGY is our main conduit to God and because of past sexual abuse many of us may have lost this conduit. Each of us needs to be healed in body, mind and Spirit. Unfortunately, for the vast majority of people, this has not happened.

Just as the music of the day tells us what is going on in society, the situations and circumstances we find ourselves in let us know what it is we need to look at and resolve. The pedophilia scandal in the Catholic Church is an indicator that we need to deal with sexual abuse issues as individuals and a nation. The vast number of children who are molested and murdered each year is another indicator that our world needs healing. It is a way of getting our attention. We must come out of denial and start to deal with sexual abuse NOW.

As a counselor I have been very blessed to have had sessions with many people over the years. Whether it was someone sitting across from me, somebody laying on my healing table with God doing the healing, or at a retreat where, as a member of a liturgical dance company, I was able to make contact with others at a soul level. Somehow when they left me they were feeling better. Funny that I didn't know what I was saying...some people call that "channeling."

I was to find out years later that my dad had molested me. Bless him for his willingness to confess it to me. My father, whom I hadn't seen for 39 years, came to live with us and during that time confessed he had molested me. What an opening and flow of energy for me! I remember thinking, "No wonder all these people have been coming to me over the years with their rape and sexual abuse issues." Now it made perfect sense. God was trying to get through to me about my own incest experiences. There was always something lying deep within my subconscious that I kept trying to bring to consciousness. Now this had finally happened! What a humbling experience. I had been able to set myself apart from others who had experienced abuse. Now all the things I had been telling them I was going to have to start telling myself and working through it as well. As I said...a truly humbling experience.

It is hard to get people to deal with the sexual abuse in their lives. Based on my own personal experience as well as those I have counseled over these 30 years, I have been given some interesting revelations. They are in the profile that follows.

There are many numbers thrown around about how many people have experienced sexual abuse. The numbers I work with come from a psychotherapists' conference held some years ago, brought together by John Bradshaw, that states close to 80% of women and 70% of men have had some form of sexual abuse by the age of 18. It is not surprising that people who haven't been sexually abused are still affected by those who have due to group consciousness.

I have found our churches have done a great disservice in making people feel guilty about their sexual energies. If our sexual energy is our main conduit to God, then it is important that we look at and become familiar with our sexual urges, and needs. We must address them and feel comfortable with them. Unfortunately, guilt and shame keep us from looking deeper. People want to get rid of parts of their body—the sexual organs—which remind them of the abuse, so they find ways of burying them. I know myself, as a dancer, I energetically pushed my pelvis into the background so I wouldn't have to deal with the abuse—even though I didn't know it had happened to me at the time.

Once when I was being interviewed on sexuality for a call in show in northern California—nobody called in! The host informed me that there was a high incidence of sexual abuse in the area. The subject matter was too close for comfort. I made a pact with myself early on in my therapy that I would deal with whatever I needed to in order to become whole. If we don't deal with it, we deal with it. What we experience is emotional pain unnecessarily.

Based on my experience, I have put together this profile of how those who have been sexually abused behave. People who have been sexually abused are:

1. Disconnected from God. Many are angry at God because they feel unprotected by Him.

2. Unable to develop healthy relationships because the person sees him/herself as deserving punishment. Domestic violence has its root cause in poor self-esteem, which causes the person to need to control their lives and everyone else in it.

3. Easily manipulated and controlled by others. They are submissive. They want to be invisible and have difficulty standing up for what is right just because they are afraid of the consequences. Speaking up is somehow linked with being sexually abused again. The memory of the sexual abuse is too painful so they want to keep it suppressed.

4. More prone to diseases of the genitals; i.e., prostate cancer, breast cancer, fibroids, uterine or cervical cancer. Because they feel those organs caused them their pain, they don't want any part of them. This additionally can cause victims to have difficulty enjoying a satisfying sexual experience. Usually they either become promiscuous or frigid and oftentimes suffer from back problems.

5. Unable to be successful at what they do.

6. Addicted to alcohol, drugs, sex, gambling, etc.

7. Lost their identity. They have to have someone in their lives at all times who will mirror to them who they are. Therefore, they don't make choices based on what they feel about a person, but how that person can fulfill their needs. Their emotional selves are very immature. They deal with things from a survival perspective. I need you – not how can we come together and create something very beautiful out of our equality and power.

8. Not able to be authentic or present; are separated from their bodies because of the abuse.

9. Become energy vampires pulling energy from others because of their lost identity.

Men have more difficulty dealing with being sexually abused because they are supposed to be the aggressors.

I had a difficult time learning to trust God. As a child I never got anything I prayed for so I believed that God hated me, and I was destined to travel this world on my own without any help from anyone. I became a survivor. For all of us learning to trust is part of the healing journey.

I have grown close to my God through my healing process. That process has taken me through years of therapy and almost every known modality of body work in this last 30 years. I have experienced many different things that have given me courage and strength for the journey. This journey can take a lifetime, but it begins with the first step. I am awake now and at peace, and I lead a happy, joyful, and fulfilling life. These are some of the things that can start the journey:

- Making a conscious decision to heal.
- Deciding to find a way to develop a relationship with God.
- Look at forgiving the person who did the molestation. On our own it is hard to do, but I can attest it is possible by asking help and guidance from the Holy Spirit, angels, God or whoever the person feels close to, for help.
- Knowing that there was a purpose for it happening helped me to look at the greater picture. Knowing they have made a conscious choice to heal in order for them to grow and also to bring about change on the planet gives meaning to what is a seeming insanity.
- Eating healthily and taking proper nutrients as well as exercising—connecting body to mind and Spirit.
- Get in for counseling with a focus on spiritual growth.
- Work with body workers to get the memories out of your cells.
- When ready, do something to help others.

When we come to a meeting of our own heart
We call—as there is a start
Of our drama which never seems to reach a comma.
It starts and stops
And stops and starts

Where is our heart
In all of this?
It's hanging out looking for a place to rest
Have we passed the test?
I don't know yet,
But at least we've met.

ONWARD ON THE JOURNEY

Clairvoyant/Alternative Health Practitioner JOY SANDERS has owned a wellness center in Simi Valley, California, for the past 19 of her 30 years in practice. She conducts health scans, past life readings, and counseling with specialties in sexual abuse and relationship issues. Visit her website: kaysnutrition.com or email kaysnv@sbcglobal.net for more information on additional products / services including her CD on sexual abuse and it's worldwide implications. (Cost: $17.95 with a $3.00 discount when mentioning this book.) Contact Joy at (805) 527-5971

CHAPTER 38

Get Intuit!

LYNN M. SCHEURELL

"The purpose of activating the intuition is that of putting at the disposal of the individual a precious function which generally remains latent and unused, thereby leaving the individual incomplete in his or her development."
—ROBERTO ASSAGIOLI

WOULD YOU LIKE to have your own personal guide to mentor you through every step you make, answer all of your questions, and show you your customized formula for life success? Of course—and you already do. The inside secret is literally within you—your own intuition.

Definition

While intuition might seem elusive, it is an integration of primal instinct, experiential life discoveries, and subconscious information that either warns us or says there's an opportunity to explore. It connects the body and the mind by communicating through spirit.

This magical internal guiding system—our intuition or inner wisdom—is physically located in two places. The small intestine is made of the same substance and secretes the same chemicals as the brain, even resembling the physical shape of the brain—the seat of our "gut" instinct. More commonly, people know of the right brain through the "third eye" between our eyebrows. Energetically, this is the sixth chakra, or seat of our "sixth sense."

We are often taught neither to follow the power of our own intuition, nor to understand that our lives are one continuous stream of our intuitive expression. This is true whether we are listening to our intuition or not. We create our lives as we live them, and regardless of our choice in denying or following our intuition, we are living with the results every day.

As humans, we filter out the familiar, becoming desensitized to our intuition. In beginning to work with our intuition, we recognize it after the fact as the proverbial thump on the head, the "Aha" moment or what we think of as coincidence. Coincidence is the manifestation of what we need to get to our next life step.

It is possible to develop our intuition "muscle." Paying attention to our inklings, the whispering of our inner voice, takes patience, commitment, and focused attention. Remember, there is no right or wrong with intuition. The real indicator of intuition is whether or not it is meaningful and supports you.

Benefits

You choose whether you follow your intuition—you hold the key to your inner guidance system. Following personal intuition has helped people make better decisions, release bad habits, and have more energy, enthusiasm, and optimism. Intuition can ease tough times and eliminate potential blocks by highlighting our negative beliefs so we can address them. Intuition allows us to understand the meaning of events in our lives, feel more relaxed and confident in our choices, and align our inner purpose with outer action. Almost magically, new channels of receptivity are opened and we attract what is right for us.

Principles

It is important to know that intuition is not judgmental. Intuition simply IS—it does not "police" our lives. In fact, it is non-resistant and will fade away in the moment if we choose to ignore it. Of course, that means our life lessons will present themselves again, often harder, but that's another topic entirely.

Intuition is ever-present; it is with us always and we can access it any time. When we do, it is dynamic, relating to where we are in the moment. The fluidity of intuition is very personal because our intuition is all about us as the sum of what we know to be true for us.

Our inner knowing is expansive. Intuition manifests tangibly in the physical world. Just look around you to know that your world is created by your intuition, the motivator of thought and action, even if unconscious. The limits on our intuition are those that our ego mind creates through internal dialogue, rationalization, and self-judgment. Our ego mind is motivated for protection; when we get information from a non-linear source, our ego mind doesn't know what to do with it and categorizes it as insufficient. So our very real internal wisdom either becomes very literal in manifestation or goes away. When we know we should take a different way to work but don't know why, our ego mind says to shake off that intuitive feeling and take the same way anyhow. Then we encounter unusual circumstances that affect us (construction, traffic, etc.). Our intuition lets us reap the consequences of our free will.

When to Listen

We don't always listen to our own intuition. In the western

world, we are socialized to look outside ourselves for messages and guidance. For some reason, credibility is external and often from someone we perceive as more powerful than ourselves. And yet, anything that comes from outside ourselves is limited because it cannot possibly know all that we know for ourselves.

When we keep getting the same message, such as a word, idea, or image from various sources, it is time to pay attention. When we know there is something bigger happening, a greater truth at work, and we need to expand our frame of reference to understand it, it's time to ask for insight. When things are going wrong, we are being gifted with energetic speed bumps, and it's time to stop, look, and listen.

Intuition is that funny feeling or sense of discomfort that doesn't make sense; a message that there's more to the situation. You may notice things are breaking or not working around you, or weird coincidences that don't really add up to what you would expect. If you feel physically ill or accidentally hurt yourself, it is time to slow down and get clarity. And if your language is "I can't take this anymore," then it's definitely time to check in with your intuition.

Language

Intuition is a "feeling" vs. an emotion; an emotion is processed through your mind, while a feeling is processed through your senses. Intuition follows your attention and intention, so more focus will yield deeper results. And personal beliefs may choose how intuition shows up for you.

We receive impressions, or fleeting insights, constantly. Impressions feel light, positive, and like energetic breathing. True intuition doesn't hurt and won't urge you to hurt others in your growth process. There is no fear in real intuition.

We humans process in pictures or images. With your eyes closed, if images come into consciousness from the right side, they are true intuitive messages. If you don't understand the picture, ask for clarity. Remember that an image could be a symbol for the true meaning. For example, a spider may mean words, a need to write or communicate.

This is also how dreams communicate with you on the astral plane. When your conscious mind is asleep, your subconscious mind is free to express your intuitive intelligence. Watch for metaphors, patterns, or hidden clues in your intuitive messages. A house is not just a house—it represents you and your body/being. A car is what takes you places—who is driving? Do you have the same dreams over and over? It helps to capture your dreams as vividly as possible upon waking, allowing you to revisit the dream's messages when you have access to conscious clarity, since we tend to lose our recall throughout the day.

Colors are important in intuitive messages and can indicate what is needed to address or resolve a situation. For a general guide, blue is self-wisdom and communication; black is new beginnings; white is intellect; purple is abundance; green is growth; red is transformation; pink is heart energy; yellow is health. If a color, or other symbol, presents and you don't know what it means, ask to understand what is being conveyed to you.

Access

When tapping into your intuition, you may feel emotional reactions, physical sensations, or ego mind chatter to block it. You may even encounter someone else's voice in your mind or a limiting belief. It is important to separate from these reactions and default programs both to minimize them and to connect with what's underneath them.

The voice of intuition is subtle. Quiet nuances and inklings are the personal precursors of truth. The little voice of inner knowledge requires attention to what's already there. Allow yourself time to be in still receptivity with eyes closed in order to get the desired information. Be transparent in your connection—cloudy thinking or hidden agendas will yield the same in return. You must ask the right question to get the right answer—and be willing to hear it.

Some people use tools to help tap into intuition, such as cards, pendulums, or other devices. However, these are not necessary to translate your soul's intuition into self-expression. Setting the space for accessing your intention need not be complicated or lengthy; it only requires focused attention.

Physically, be present and grounded in your body in a comfortable environment. Acknowledge your readiness, expand your consciousness, and relax in the knowingness that it will happen. Suspend any judgment or attachment to a particular outcome, as your intuition may guide you in something you may not think you want and may therefore be blocked. Set your intention to attune your consciousness for clarity and open channels to receive messages.

When you are ready to access your intuition, think the word "yes." Pay attention to how "yes" resonates in your body, how you feel and perceive it, if there is a color or image associated with it. When you have anchored how "yes" feels for you, repeat the process with the word "no" until you understand what "no" is for you. The next step is to ask clarifying questions about your issue or challenge, or to make "as if" statements, and feel them according to your "yes/no" scale. A "yes" may even pull your body forward slightly as a "no" pushes back. If you get a mushy or unclear answer, more information is needed. You decide how much time to spend; remember, intuition is available to you at any time.

Drains

In developing and accessing your intuition, it is important to avoid being self-critical in any way. While it may feel natural to scoff at, feel confused, or dismiss the results as coincidence, each is taking power away from your intuition. Feeling "too" sensitive or in a state of overwhelm will block the flow of intuitive messages as well. Intuition is a natural guide and responds to your state of receptivity; if you aren't open, you won't hear it.

Other drains include negative people and negative thoughts. It is universal law that what we focus on expands, and that includes giving energy to negativity or negative people. To minimize negativity, direct your attention elsewhere, including not doing "the work" for other people. It is not up to us to take away others' opportunities to learn their life lessons. That simply drains your intuition on their behalf and serves neither.

What Next?

Remember to look inside first to get answers. Know and trust what you know, regardless of how a situation may appear. Develop discernment to know what is true for you, and make decisions accordingly. It is impossible to unlearn what you learn – and action is being responsible with your life. If you ignore your intuition, you could experience blockages, a lack of flow, and a chance to re-address the underlying issue later anyway, and in a usually exaggerated, experience. So get out of your way and let your intuition be your best life guide!

LYNN SCHEURELL'S life focus is facilitating positive transformation in the lives she touches, which includes hundreds of clients. For most of her life, she limited her intuitive expression, not understanding that it is only by living according to one's individual truths that one can live in the flow. Her company, Creative Catalyst, is a leader in initiating intuitive life change for independent professionals and business owners throughout the United States. You can reach her at MyCreativeCatalyst.com.

CHAPTER 39

The Art of Healing the Spirit:
One Woman's Journey
LYNDA SCHLOSBERG

IT'S A GRAY WINTER DAY and I'm on the highway somewhere in Connecticut. I just finished looking at a high-end printer for my photography. I'm lost in excitement with the possibilities this new technology will bring, when I roll-up behind a long line of cars with their emergency flashers on. It's a funeral procession. I've been inside one of those cars far too many times in the last several years. A flood of memories fills my head—the day my only sister Carol was murdered; losing Robert, the man I loved, in a plane crash…I recall the excruciating pain and heartache, I reflect on all that I have endured, and realize how far I have come.

Experiencing the death of a loved one inherently brings into view our own mortality. It makes us ask, "Why am I here? And what am I doing about it?" Other kinds of loss also make us ask the same questions. Divorce, the end of an intimate relationship, the loss of a job, children growing up and leaving home, reaching mid-life or facing retirement can all make us pose the question "What is the purpose of my life?"

Whatever the loss may be, a common reaction is to jump into something new or make radical and outward changes to your life. It could include diving into a new relationship, quitting your job, moving to a new location, taking up a sport or hobby, losing weight or going back to school. I did many of those things. I quit my high paying corporate job and started my own business. Changed the color of my hair (a couple of times). Moved three times in three years. Lost weight and took up swimming and long-distance cycling. My focus was on outward concrete activities that, while producing very tangible and valuable results, still left me feeling 'flat.' Something was missing. The reality was, my life was controlling me, and I was just reacting to it. I had neither found nor healed my spirit, and I was no closer to understanding what my life was really all about.

There are lots of excellent self-help books out there that provide good ideas on how to heal yourself and find meaning to your life, but what I discovered is that the process for healing is completely unique to you. No one book, class or theory is going to be a silver bullet for your healing. Instead it is a cumulative process you have to figure out for yourself as you go. Since you are the only one who has direct access to your inner soul—or spirit—you are the only one who can craft your personal plan to heal.

It may mean trying lots of different things and going down a path only to find you need to turn around, go back, and pick a different one to try. It might mean opening yourself up to different experiences until you find the one, or several, that is right for you. I also learned it's a process that takes time, requiring patience, dedication and hard work. But before long, you may begin noticing shifts in your life—signs that confirm you're moving in the right direction.

My journey towards healing was a long one that started by going deep inside myself to find my spirit then learning how to hear it and letting it guide me to my future. Looking back on my experience I realize there were a few significant, simultaneously occurring elements that played critical roles in my healing and self-discovery.

ELEMENT ONE: FIND YOUR SPIRIT

For any major shift to occur, I realized it was essential to be aware of my own belief system. How could I heal my spirit if I didn't know what my spirit was?

After Robert died I desperately wanted to know what happened to him. Was his spirit 'energetically' out there somewhere? Or was his spirit just the memory of him in my heart? Because I didn't have a solid belief system, I didn't have the answers to those questions. So I read dozens of books, went to a series of psychics, saw a therapist regularly, learned about energy healing, took a class on mediumship, meditated, prayed and filled several journals with every thought in my head.

I investigated, questioned, probed and poked holes in all my theories. Until one day, I realized somewhere along the line, through all my research and questioning, I had actually found my faith. And once I allowed myself to truly believe in it—almost as if in an instant—my spirit was completely healed.

ELEMENT TWO: LISTEN TO YOUR INNER VOICE

I also recognized in order to find and be in connection with my spirit meant learning how to turn down the volume on the daily chatter in my head and turn up the volume on my inner voice. I did this by shutting off the TV and car stereo. I took long silent walks around Walden Pond, and when I didn't have much time I'd just take a walk around the block. I learned how to meditate and wrote in a journal every morning. I found the more time I spent alone with my thoughts and emotions, the better I could hear the voice of my inner spirit revealing my core values, motivating factors and operating principles. As I paid closer attention to what it was saying, I began to act upon its guidance, which helped me to find the reason for my being.

ELEMENT THREE: UNCOVER YOUR PASSION

While I participated in many activities I enjoyed and made me feel good, I still felt as though I was wandering a bit aimlessly through life. I didn't feel connected to anything bigger, something more meaningful. After my sister died I was given a pocket digital camera. I went on long walks to be alone with my thoughts (turning up the volume on my inner voice), and I took pictures of anything that interested me along the way. They were just snapshots, but the process of taking them was healing for me. Sharing them with people I loved was even more healing. Oddly enough it became healing for them too.

Pretty soon the long walks were less about my thoughts and more about the photos I was taking.

One spring afternoon I took a shot of a white peony, and as I downloaded the image onto my computer, I couldn't believe what I saw. My spirit was looking right back at me through this photograph. It was in that precise moment that it all became crystal clear—my life was about combining my lifelong love for photography and art with healing. By allowing the space to hear my spirit I found my passion, connecting me to something bigger and more universal than myself, and giving real meaning to my life.

ELEMENT FOUR: MAINTAIN PATIENCE AND TRUST

I learned to pay attention to—and trust—the synchronistic and cumulative events that began to occur. They weren't coincidences. It was my spirit nudging me in the direction of my life path. Once I started acting on them, I began to experience profound changes.

Writing this chapter is a perfect example. A short while ago I had an intense vision that writing a book on my experiences of loss and recovery was in my future. Three weeks later the opportunity to be in this book presented itself. This wasn't an accident—it was a synchronistic event that I knew to act upon. Not only has writing this chapter fueled ideas for a future book, it has opened me up to other broader possibilities, nudging me closer to my proper destiny.

As part of this process I learned patience. Even when I felt as if I wasn't getting anywhere—I was. One small thing would shift, and suddenly everything would fall perfectly into place, and I'd make a huge leap forward. Then the process would start all over again. Moments of insight and clarity came like waves from the ocean, one building on the next until it all made sense and I had 'arrived.' My spirit was healed, and I had discovered the real reason to my life. The choices I now make have absolute clarity and focus. I feel complete and whole. Nothing is missing anymore.

Amazingly I am happier now than I have ever been. Ironically I wouldn't be in this state of bliss had I not suffered such deep loss and pain. It has occurred because I consciously chose to take advantage of the process of my own healing.

The journey of finding and healing my spirit was enormously profound and deep. It has provided me with pure contentment, total fulfillment, complete empowerment over my life, and a reminder of what unconditional love is really all about. It is a state of utter joy that I wish for everyone. I wish it for you.

LYNDA SCHLOSBERG is a professional graphic designer, fine-art photographer and Reconnective Healing practitioner. After her own experiences with sudden and tragic loss, she embarked on an eight-year journey towards healing. During her process of self-discovery, she uncovered a creative path for finding her spirit, which she shares with others to help in their personal healing and fulfillment. For creative exercises and inspiration on how to help heal your spirit visit www.artofhealingspirit.com.

CHAPTER 40

The Power of a Values-Driven Life

RAQUEL SMITH

WOULD YOU LIKE TO ACHIEVE success in all areas of your life? Do you feel like you are compromising your values on a daily basis? Are you in a job just to pay the bills with no fulfillment? If you answered yes to any of these questions then this chapter will provide you with a toolbox of strategies to enable you to live the life of your dreams. You can eliminate all these situations from your life by aligning your values with your goals and dreams. You can live a life of integrity and massive abundance.

First off, in order to have integrity you need to know what your values are. Defining your values will lead you to a path of integrity. Values are the things that influence how you live your life. Values are expressed by actions not mere words. Unfortunately, many go through life in a fog, just living the way you were "trained" to live through the values that were passed down to you through family, friends, society, and your environment.

You may be going through life just living day to day without thought or focus on what you are pursuing. You sometimes wonder why you are unable to be successful at your endeavors. You feel stuck or even feel like you are on life's roller coaster with no chance of getting off. You may have a burst of success, but there are more down times than up. This may leave you in a state of depression, ready to give up except you can't afford to.

The good news is there is hope! You can be unstuck! You can live a successful life and enjoy the journey. Believe it or not, you have all the resources right at your fingertips. You just need to reach out and grab them. You may say, "I have tried many things and nothing works." I am sure you have, but you have been trying things that were not aligned with your personal values. You cannot succeed without walking the path of your values. Aligning your values with your goals and dreams will propel you to the life of success that you have always yearned for! You will be surprised that moving just one step towards being aligned with your values will cause a big improvement in your life.

The reason why success seems to be unreachable is because you are not doing what you value. In other words, you are working a job or are in a career that is paying the bills, but you are unfulfilled because you are just chasing the almighty dollar. This is not getting you anywhere near your goals and dreams.

A values driven life will automatically empower you to be successful. You will even have a more successful relationship with your significant other. You are saying, "How is that possible?" Well, once you define your values, then you will know what your relationship values are. In so doing, you will find a partner who has similar values as yourself. Then, you can both work on aligning your individual values as a couple and even define values for the relationship itself. A successful relationship is built on both parties having similar values. Once you take a moment to define your values, you will see the right direction to take in your life, and you will not hesitate to follow your passion.

Aligning your values with your goals will infuse your life with the needed passion to do, be, and create whatever you want. You will no longer settle for less, but will instead walk the path of your destiny. Your values will be so embedded you will not think twice about doing anything that will go against them. I am sure you have heard that whatever you do, do it with passion. The reason being, without passion, you will not be as successful because you are not putting your all into it.

Some people may confuse habit with values. A habit is something that is done constantly on a regular basis. In your mind, you may say that you value something because you do it everyday. A habit is not necessarily a value. For example, you may regularly hang out with a certain crowd. Hanging out with these people is not something you value, however, you developed the habit just to be a part of the group.

Picture a young kid who grew up in a low-income family. He only knew about lack and scarcity. However, that kid loved to read and soon learned that there was another world outside of where he lived. The kid grew up to be a somewhat responsible man. He tried his hand at many different jobs and just about anything. All this was done in his pursuit of trying to be successful and to live a comfortable life. But try as he did, he could never seem to find the right way out of his predicament. Once in a while he got lucky at making some "good money" but that only lasted for what seemed like a short time.

He read personal development books and even became a seminar junkie. He would go to every seminar that he could in hopes of "fixing" himself. To his dismay, he would be right back at square one once the seminar was over. One day he was talking to a friend and the friend invited him to go to a seminar entitled "My Values, My Life." Even though he was a bit hesitant after attending so many seminars before, he decided to go.

At the seminar he discovered he was living his life based on what he saw happen in his family. He was working under his family's values of scarcity and lack. He realized he would never be a success if he continued in this situation. He learned that day that he must define his personal values and live his values in order to achieve his dreams.

He took the opportunity the speaker gave to participate in a free session on defining values. After the session he was totally changed; he discovered his values did not allow him to participate in lack. He was able to align his values with his goals and dreams and found out that he could live his dreams in vibrant colors. He was able to become a successful consultant and live in total abundance. This was only possible because he aligned his values, which allowed him to pursue his passion without chasing the dollar in a merry-go-round.

Here are the steps to defining your values; it should be done with a coach preferably for a more in-depth process and better results:

1. Ask yourself, "What is truly important to me in life?"

2. List the answers on a sheet of paper. Each response should only be a word or two to capture the essence.

3. Prioritize your list, starting from the top value to the least. Do this by asking yourself which one of these values is most important to you if you could only have one. Keep doing this until the list is completely prioritized.

4. Look at the prioritized list, and you will see your personal values for life. You will feel the connection with those values. You will know what you value most in life.

5. You will begin to align your behavior with your values.

6. You will begin to make your decisions based on your values. When you have a decision to make you will consult your values list and choose the path that is aligned with your values.

You can now agree with me that aligning your values with your goals and dreams is one of the most powerful things you can do to lead you to the road of success. You will not look back. Your life will be on track and on purpose. Everyone will be saying, "There is something different about you; I just can't put a finger on it." You will just smile because you know your values are aligned with your goals and dreams and you can't help but be successful. You know your life is empowered with success because you are living a values driven life.

RAQUEL SMITH, Values Alignment Coach™ is a Certified Master Results Coach, certified in Creation Technologies©. Raquel specializes in values alignment, which builds integrity and a life of success and abundance. Raquel has extensive experience in people relations and coaching to success. Raquel's company, Golden Life Coaching does one-on-one, couples and group sessions and seminars. You may contact (866) 394-3081 or email info@goldenlifecoaching.com for more information. To subscribe to the monthly newsletter and to receive a free audio download, go to www.goldenlifecoaching.com.

CHAPTER 41

Be Careful What You Wish For...Oops! You've Already Got It

ANNETTA WILSON

A FRIEND ONCE TOLD ME, "I can't believe how the universe responds to you!" He was convinced I lived under a lucky star. At the time I didn't fully appreciate his insight. But I did start paying attention...attention to my thoughts and prayers. The most amazing thing happened! I realized the undeniable connection between my 'thought' life and my reality.

I decided to consciously work at connecting the dots. This began a wonderful game God and I still play: I make a wish, hold tight to that vision and trust that He'll do the rest. He lets me win most of the time. When I don't win, the 'why' usually becomes clear with time (followed by my undying gratitude and sigh of relief that I didn't get my wish).

I'm not implying that God is a genie in a bottle or some cosmic fairy godmother. He simply agrees with us when we decide how to think about, wish for, and envision the events in our lives. The unnerving side effect is that it takes all the fun out of playing the victim.

Whether you accept it or deny it, you are creating your future each day with every thought, every wish, every prayer and every desire you send into the universe. If you're like most people you need proof. I can't give the proof you may need for your life. You'll have to take that journey yourself. I can only tell you my story.

THE CAREER THAT ROSE LIKE
A PHOENIX FROM THE ASHES:

I sat watching the midday news with my infant son in my lap. On the air, by my former co-anchor's side, was another woman. Why was she there? Why was she in my anchor chair? I had worked with this man for years. We were a team. At least we had been a team years earlier.

I had put my career as a television news anchor on hold to move out of state with my husband. Now, three and a half years later, we were back in Orlando with a new baby, and I had chosen to stay at home with my son. I don't regret my decision to this day, but I never let go of the vision that someday I'd be back in my old anchor chair. In reality, the odds of me getting my job back after taking that much time off were slim to none, and 'Slim' had just left town. I wasn't in the business anymore.

Fast-forward three years. Through old connections, I began working as a vacation fill-in anchor at another television station. It wasn't steady, but it was a start. I'd also had my second child by this point. After about a year, I was offered a full-time job, but I never forgot about my old anchor chair or my old station. By this time however, it was just a passing 'what if?'

Meanwhile, things were changing at my current job. My boss was trying to hold onto her job and didn't know where mine would fit in with the new changes. I remember sitting in my office with the door closed and the lights off. It was time for one of my heart-to-heart talks with God. I asked Him why He would let me get so close to getting my career back and then allow it to all go up in smoke. What I didn't know was that His plan was already in motion.

A few days after my closed-door session with God, I got a call from a woman I'd worked with years earlier at my former station. She had been asked to come back and revive their community affairs department. She wasn't interested, but thought I'd be perfect for the job. We set up a meeting with the new head of the station.

After rounds of interviews with other candidates, he offered me the job. Now, 12 years after I had left, I was back at my old station, this time in management. Guess what? My former co-anchor was still there!

I settled comfortably into my new role. One day the news director called me into his office. He'd had a brainstorm and wanted to make me a proposition. He wanted to know if I wanted to anchor again, with Ben!

He envisioned a 'They're back together again' campaign. All he needed was for me to say yes. I would not have to give up my management position, and there would be additional compensation.

After a 12-year gap, two children, starting my career again almost from ground zero and never losing sight of my wish, I proudly sat down next to Ben in 'my' anchor chair. We were a team once again and remained so until he retired. I had done it! With God's guidance and a vision I refused to relinquish, my wish had come true. My career was on its way back up. Unfortunately, my marriage didn't survive the transition.

I came to understand that timetables are not mine. They belong to God. My job was to prepare and be ready when the opportunities presented themselves.

That lesson would prove itself again a few years later when I met my new husband.

THE MAN I (THOUGHT) I DESIGNED:

My children were now six and nine. I was divorced from their father and building a new life for them and for myself. A trip to New Orleans would forever change how I looked at relationships.

My brother, sister, and I decided to spend July 4th weekend at the Essence Music Festival. I was excited about the concerts, empowerment workshops, and the flavor of the 'Big Easy.' What I didn't expect was the impact one of those workshops would have on my life. In a very real sense one particular workshop was the first step on the path that led me to my husband.

The speaker (Iyanla Vanzant) had the all-female audience spellbound. She told us that the lovers we had in our lives were people we'd 'called' into our lives. She told us in order to get something or someone different, we had to be specific with God about what we wanted. She told us to make a list. I was listening.

Before that moment, it had never occurred to me that I could apply the same 'wish' method to my personal life that I had applied to my career. I needed to see if it worked with matters of the heart.

I got back home after that weekend and began making my list. I knew enough about God to understand I couldn't be flippant about the process. I said a prayer, stilled my heart and began writing. The first thing on my list was 'loves and honors God.' I realized if this key component was missing, nothing else on the list mattered.

I really got into it. The list ran the gamut from 'has no emotional attachment to another woman' to 'loves kids' to 'great sense of humor.' Of course I threw in the requisite tall, dark, and handsome. I figured I might as well go for broke!

I'd love to tell you that I met him right away. I didn't. It took four years. God is always on time...but not necessarily on our timetable. I definitely kissed a couple of frogs before I found my prince. But I did find him. We met as a result of a dare from a friend, email exchanges, and a blind date.

I had forgotten about my 'wish' list. I only thought about it when I came across it in the place in my Bible where it was safely tucked away. In the meantime, I was enjoying getting to know this man who was slowly and imperceptibly checking off every single item on my list.

As is God's pattern with me, the fact that my 'wish' list had been fulfilled hit me like a ton of bricks...while I was heading out the door for church one day.

As I hurriedly grabbed my Bible, my list fell out of its hiding place onto the floor. I picked up the four-year-old piece of paper, read it, and looked at the man I was to marry as if I were seeing him for the first time. Standing in front of me in the flesh was every single thing I had asked of God.

He looked at the list I handed to him and, with his warped sense of humor, patted himself on the back for being such an incredible catch. To this day he reminds me that I 'ordered him up.'

What I've learned from these two experiences is that I already have the things that make up my thoughts, hopes, wishes, dreams, and prayers. And yes, I still play my little game with God, and He still lets me win!

ANNETTA WILSON is a talent coach for CNN. She's a business strategist specializing in media training for interview preparation, message development, and crisis communication. Annetta also coaches individuals who want more "Aha!" moments in their lives. An award-winning journalist, she's worked in the broadcast industry over 30 years. She counts Walt Disney World among her clients. Log onto www.YourCoachForSuccess.com for free tips. Contact Annetta at (407) 333-4744 or ContactUs@YourCoachForSuccess.com.

ABOUT THE AUTHORS

The women who contributed to this book come from diverse backgrounds and have mastered a wide range of skills and approaches. They are executives, relationship experts, educators, psychotherapists, trainers, doctors, coaches, healers and more. Many have worked for enterprises ranging from Fortune 500 companies to small businesses, though most are now entrepreneurs. The one thing that unites them is success. Every one of them has demonstrated passion and excellence in their endeavors. How can we know this? Results. Though you might not recognize the names instantly, many of these women have been featured on national television and in national magazines. They all have something to say worth knowing. Together they have contributed to a book that is greater than the sum of its parts.

ABOUT CHRISTINE KLOSER

Christine Kloser, Author, President of Love Your Life Publishing and Founder of NEW Entrepreneurs, Inc. is an entrepreneur extraordinaire. Christine has coached, advised and inspired thousands of women to take charge of their personal, financial, spiritual and business lives. She is a pioneer in bridging the gap between business and spirituality.

Christine has been a guest on numerous local and national radio and TV shows and her articles and quotes appear in a variety of publications including *Entrepreneur Magazine, Palisadian Post, The Argonaut, She Ink,* and *Woman's Day.* She has also been featured in the books, *What Nobody Ever Tells You About Starting Your Own Business, Web Wonder Women, Heart of a Woman, Visionary Women, Empowering Women to Power Network,* and *Secrets of the Millionaire Mind.* A proud member of the Who's Who of Empowering Executives and Professionals, Christine was also recognized for winning the 2004 Wealthy Woman "Business Ambassador" Award for her dedication to empowering women entrepreneurs.

This book extends the benefits of her creativity and experience to women around the world.

Christine conducts business bi-coastally. She lives in Pennsylvania with her husband and daughter.

To learn more about Christine Kloser, please contact her at:

Christine Kloser
c/o Love Your Life Publishing
PO Box 661274
Los Angeles, CA 90066
Ph: (310) 962-4710
Fax: (310) 496-0716
Email: publish@loveyourlife.com
Web: www.loveyourlife.com

Network for Empowering Women
Helping Women Ignite Their Business And Fuel Their Soul™

Christine Kloser started NEW Entrepreneurs, Inc. in 2000 when she gathered with five friends in the back of a Chinese Restaurant. She had a vision to create a small group of like-minded women who would support each other in entrepreneurial and personal success. That small group has since grown to serve thousands of women world-wide through NEW Connections Ezine, Virtual Meetings, Live Networking Events, Retreats, and most recently a publishing division (Love Your Life Publishing).

You're invited to "get connected to NEW" with
NEW Connections Ezine.

You'll receive FREE Tips, Tools and Resources to turn your "inspirations into realizations!"

NEW Connections is your complete resource for business, spiritual, personal and financial fulfillment.

HERE'S HOW YOU'LL BENEFIT:

- Get invitations to FREE events with leading business and success experts
- Discover resources that save you time and money
- Learn new strategies for boosting your bottom line
- Find out how you can have it all
- And much more

Go to: www.NewNewsletter.com

You'll receive more than $2,000 in bonus gifts when you subscribe.

NEW Connections is a bi-weekly online publication brought to you by NEW Entrepreneurs, Inc., www.NEWentrepreneurs.com.

Do you have a book inside you?

Most people do.

Just like the contributors to this book, you can see your words in print in six months or less.

Take our short quiz at
www.LoveYourLife.com/authorquiz
to find out if you're ready to get published.

Love Your Life Publishing is your publishing partner specializing in high quality compilation books.

Love Your Life Publishing
PO Box 661274
Los Angeles, CA 90066
Ph: (310) 962-4710
Fax: (310) 496-0716
Email: publish@loveyourlife.com
Web: www.loveyourlife.com

Also by Love Your Life Publishing:

Stepping Up to the Plate:
Inspiring Interviews with Major Leaguers
By David Kloser
ISBN: 0-9664806-2-7

Inspiration to Realization – Volume I:
Real Women Reveal Proven Strategies for
Personal, Business, Financial and Spiritual Fulfillment
ISBN: 0-9664806-3-5

Inspiration to Realization – Volume II:
Real Women Reveal Proven Strategies for
Personal, Business, Financial and Spiritual Fulfillment
ISBN: 0-9664806-4-3

Love Your Life books may be purchased
for educational, business or sales and promotion use.

For information, please write:
Love Your Life Publishing
PO Box 661274
Los Angeles, CA 90066

Email: Publish@loveyourlife.com
Visit: www.loveyourlife.com
Phone: (310)962-4710